REVIVAL

REVIVAL

Spiritual Awakening in the Reformed Tradition

Michael A. G. Azad Haykin

Reformation Heritage Books
Grand Rapids, Michigan

Revival
© 2024 by Michael A. G. Azad Haykin

All rights reserved. No part of this book may be used or reproduced in any manner whatsoever without written permission except in the case of brief quotations embodied in critical articles and reviews. Direct your requests to the publisher at the following addresses:

Reformation Heritage Books
3070 29th St. SE
Grand Rapids, MI 49512
616-977-0889
orders@heritagebooks.org
www.heritagebooks.org

Scripture taken from the King James Version. In the public domain.

Printed in the United States of America
24 25 26 27 28 29/10 9 8 7 6 5 4 3 2 1

Library of Congress Cataloging-in-Publication Data

Names: Haykin, Michael A. G., author.
Title: Revival : spiritual awakening in the Reformed tradition / Michael A.G. Azad Haykin.
Description: Grand Rapids, Michigan : Reformation Heritage Books, [2024] | Includes bibliographical references.
Identifiers: LCCN 2023050461 (print) | LCCN 2023050462 (ebook) | ISBN 9798886860962 (paperback) | ISBN 9798886860979 (epub)
Subjects: LCSH: Church renewal—Reformed Church—History.
Classification: LCC BV600.3 .H446 2024 (print) | LCC BV600.3 (ebook) | DDC 269/.24—dc23/eng/20231220
LC record available at https://lccn.loc.gov/2023050461
LC ebook record available at https://lccn.loc.gov/2023050462

For additional Reformed literature, request a free book list from Reformation Heritage Books at the above regular or email address.

To Joel Beeke,

with deep thanks to God for his friendship
and fellowship in the gospel.

"There is no subject which is of greater importance to the Christian church at the present time than that of revival. It should be the theme of our constant meditation, preaching and prayers."
—D. Martyn Lloyd-Jones

"I am an eighteenth-century man."
—D. Martyn Lloyd-Jones

Contents

Introduction xi

1. "When the Spirit Shall Be Poured Forth Plentifully": Revival in the Reformation and English Puritanism 1
2. "God Is Doing Marvellous Things": The British Need for and Experience of Revival in the Eighteenth Century 17
3. "Come to This Life-Giving Stream": George Whitefield and His Ministry in a Time of Revival 33
4. "He Carries Fire Wherever He Goes": William Grimshaw and the Haworth Revival 55
5. "The Theologian of Revival": Becoming Jonathan Edwards ... 69
6. "A Spirit of Powerful Holy Affection": Twelve Marks of Genuine Revival 83
7. "We Are a Garden Wall'd Around": Particular Baptists Needing Revival 99
8. "Impress Thy Truth upon My Heart with Thine Own Seal": Andrew Fuller and Theological Reformation 115
9. "The Lord Is Doing Great Things, and Answering Prayer Every Where": John Sutcliff and the Concert of Prayer for Revival 131

Conclusion: Eight Theses on Revival 147

Appendix 1: William Grimshaw's Letter on the Haworth Revival 151

Appendix 2: John Stutterd, "The Means of Reviving and Promoting Religion" 155

Acknowledgments 167

Introduction

This small book on revival, one of thousands that have been written on this vital subject, is written with the conviction that I learned from Martyn Lloyd-Jones and that was reinforced by Richard Lovelace: the history of the church is a history of revival, "a history of ups and downs."[1] To record that entire history would require a good number of volumes. The aim of this book is far more modest. It seeks to stoke the passion, as it were, for the presence of Christ's Spirit of revival by looking at two moments in this history of renewal: the transatlantic Great Awakening in the mid-eighteenth-century Anglo-American world and the revival of the Particular Baptists in the British and Irish archipelago at the close of the eighteenth century, which stands at the fountainhead of what historians term the Second Great Awakening. In many ways, years of study of revival and renewal have convinced me that these two scenes of church history are paradigmatic when it comes to the subject of revival.

The first chapter contains a number of snapshots of the way that revival was a feature of both the Reformation and English Puritanism. In essence, it seeks to show that concern for revival was not unheard of prior to the awakenings of the eighteenth century. After detailing the need for revival in eighteenth-century Great Britain and highlighting the revivals that took place in Wales and Scotland, we then look at three key figures of the First Great Awakening: George

---

1. D. Martyn Lloyd-Jones, *Revival* (Westchester, IL: Crossway, 1987), 26. See also Richard F. Lovelace, *Dynamics of Spiritual Life: An Evangelical Theology of Renewal* (Downers Grove, IL: InterVarsity Press, 1978).

Whitefield, William Grimshaw, and Jonathan Edwards. Above all figures, Whitefield brought together the various revivals in the United Kingdom and her American colonies. Grimshaw is a good case study of what revival looked like in a local parish. Edwards, while ministering in the somewhat different context of the British colonies in America, provided the First Great Awakening on both sides of the Atlantic with a paradigmatic theology of revival. While these three men are not without their weaknesses and faults—the subject of slavery in the cases of Whitefield and Edwards is a clear and recent example—their experience of and thinking about revival forms, in the opinion of this author, are a standard in many ways as we think about and long for revival. The second half of the book, chapters 6 to 9, looks at the revival of a community of Baptists, the Particular Baptists in Great Britain and Ireland. After also detailing the way that this community needed reviving (a chapter that parallels chapter 2, which sketches the need for revival prior to the First Great Awakening), we look at two key figures in this Baptist revival, Andrew Fuller and John Sutcliff, and their distinct contributions to this time of renewal.

It is obvious that far more could be said about revival. I think of studies that I have done and lectures that I have given on Asahel Nettleton, the Haldanes, *le Réveil* among the French Calvinistic churches in the nineteenth century, and the revival of the Gaelic-speaking Baptist churches of the Ottawa Valley, Ontario, in the 1830s. And while there are a number of works available that deal with the overall history of revival,[2] my approach is to focus on a couple of major revivals so as to discern a number of key principles with regard to revival.[3] Again, let me stress, the revivals considered in this book, which are

---

2. See, for example, R. E. Davies, *I Will Pour Out My Spirit: A History and Theology of Revivals and Evangelical Awakenings* (Tunbridge Wells, Kent: Monarch Publications, 1992). See also the fine studies of revival by Eifion Evans, *Fire in the Thatch: The True Nature of Religious Revival* (Bryntirion, Bridgend: Evangelical Press of Wales, 1996) and by Brian H. Edwards, *Revival: A People Saturated with God* (Leominster: Day One Publications, 2019).

3. For a focused approach to revival similar to what I am doing in this book, see Ian Randall's excellent work, *Rhythms of Revival: The Spiritual Awakening of 1857–1863* (Milton Keynes: Paternoster, 2010).

from what historians call the "long eighteenth century" (the 1680s to the 1810s, or even to the 1830s), provide a template or paradigm for our thinking about revival. Hopefully, what this book outlines about revival will provide principles about this all-important subject and stimulate ardent prayer for God to revive His church in the midst of these trying times.[4]

St. David's Day, 2022
Dundas, Ontario

---

4. See the Conclusion for a summary of these principles in the form of eight theses.

CHAPTER 1

"When the Spirit Shall Be Poured Forth Plentifully"

Revival in the Reformation and English Puritanism

The renewal of interest in Reformed teaching and doctrine over the past sixty years has been tremendous. A key means by which this interest has been kindled and enabled to flourish has been the British Westminster Conference (formerly known as the Puritan Conference). Organized in the 1950s by, among others, Martyn Lloyd-Jones (1899–1981) and J. I. Packer (1926–2020), this conference, which still meets annually in December, has played a vital role in awakening evangelicals to the riches of Puritan and Reformed theology. For many years it was customary for Lloyd-Jones to give the final address of the conference. The first of such addresses was the one that he gave in 1959 entitled "Revival: An Historical and Theological Survey."[1] Lloyd-Jones began his address by defining revival as "an experience in the life of the church when the Holy Spirit does an unusual work." These extraordinary movements of the Spirit consist first of all, he stated, in the "enlivening and quickening and awakening of lethargic, sleeping, almost moribund church members" and then in "the conversion of masses of people who hitherto have been outside in indifference and in sin."[2] Lloyd-Jones went on to illustrate his definition of revival from the history of the church and from Scripture and to show that "the history of the progress and development of the church is largely a history of revivals...these mighty exceptional effusions of the Spirit of God." What is striking about Lloyd-Jones's survey

---

1. For the full address, see D. M. Lloyd-Jones, *The Puritans: Their Origins and Successors: Addresses Delivered at the Puritan and Westminster Conferences 1959–1978* (Edinburgh: Banner of Truth, 1987), 1–23.

2. Lloyd-Jones, *Puritans*, 1–2.

of the history of revival is the significant place that revivals have occupied in the Reformed tradition. Lloyd-Jones asserted that one of the main reasons why revivals have not been prominent in the past century is due to the fact that the final half of the nineteenth century witnessed a widespread turning away from Reformed theology which continued unabated until the late 1940s.[3]

To those acquainted with the history of Calvinism these assertions by Lloyd-Jones should not be a surprise. For instance, the massive advance of the gospel in Europe during the time of the Reformation can be adequately explained only in terms of spiritual revival. And on the cutting edge of this advance were undoubtedly those whom today we call Calvinists (though, it should be noted, John Calvin would abhor the use of this term). Consider France as an example. It has been estimated that by the time of John Calvin's death in 1564 there were roughly 1,200 Reformed congregations in the country with around two million members, which was about a tenth of France's population.[4] And the emergence of these congregations occurred in the space of less than fifty years! But let us focus our attention on Puritan thinking about revival.

A deep and abiding interest in the work of the Holy Spirit lies at the very core of English Puritanism, that late sixteenth- and seventeenth-century movement that sought to reform the Church of England and, failing to do so, splintered into a variety of denominations such as English Presbyterian, Congregationalist, Particular (i.e., Calvinistic) and General (i.e., Arminian) Baptist.[5] Whatever else the Puritans may have been—social, political, and ecclesiastical Reformers—they were primarily men and women intensely passionate about piety and Christian experience. By and large united in their Calvinism, the Puritans believed that every aspect of their spiritual lives came from the work of the Holy Spirit. They had in fact

---

3. Lloyd-Jones, *Puritans*, 4–5.
4. Mark Greengrass, *The French Reformation* (Oxford: Basil Blackwell, Ltd., 1987), 43.
5. Irvonwy Morgan, *Puritan Spirituality* (London: Epworth Press, 1973), 53–65; Dewey D. Wallace, Jr., *The Spirituality of the Later English Puritans: An Anthology* (Macon, GA: Mercer University Press, 1987), xi–xiv; J. I. Packer, *A Quest for Godliness: The Puritan Vision of the Christian Life* (Wheaton, IL: Crossway Books, 1990), 37–38.

inherited from the continental Reformers of the sixteenth century, and from John Calvin (1506–1564) in particular, "a constant and even distinctive concern" with the person and work of the Holy Spirit.[6] Benjamin B. Warfield (1851–1921), the distinguished American Presbyterian theologian, can actually speak of Calvin as "preeminently the theologian of the Holy Spirit."[7] And about his Puritan heirs and their interest in the Holy Spirit, Warfield has this to say:

> The formulation of the doctrine of the work of the Spirit waited for the Reformation and for Calvin, and…the further working out of the details of this doctrine and its enrichment by the profound study of Christian minds and meditation of Christian hearts has come down from Calvin only to the Puritans…. It is only the truth to say that Puritan thought was almost entirely occupied with loving study of the work of the Holy Spirit, and found its highest expression in dogmatico-practical expositions of the several aspects of it.[8]

Here are four vignettes of revival in the Puritan era.

Dedham, Essex[9]

When John Rogers (ca. 1570–1636) first went up to Emmanuel College, Cambridge, as a student in February 1588 he proved to be a complete wastrel. His way was being paid by his uncle, the well-known Puritan preacher Richard Rogers (1551–1618), but John sold all of his books so as to spend the proceeds on various sinful activities. Not surprisingly,

---

6. Richard B. Gaffin, "The Holy Spirit," *The Westminster Theological Journal* 43 (1980): 61. See also the detailed discussion by Garth B. Wilson, "Doctrine of the Holy Spirit in the Reformed Tradition: A Critical Overview," in George Vandervelde, ed., *The Holy Spirit: Renewing and Empowering Presence* (Winfield, BC: Wood Lake Books, 1989), 57–62.

7. Benjamin B. Warfield, "Calvin's Doctrine of the Knowledge of God" in Samuel G. Craig, ed., *Calvin and Augustine* (repr., Phillipsburg, NJ: Presbyterian and Reformed Publishing Co., 1980), 107. See also his "John Calvin: The Man and His Work" and "John Calvin the Theologian," in Craig, ed., *Calvin and Augustine*, 21, 487.

8. Benjamin B. Warfield, "Introductory Note" to Abraham Kuyper, *The Work of the Holy Spirit*, trans. Henri de Vries (1900; Grand Rapids: Eerdmans, 1956) xxxv, xxviii.

9. For some of the following discussion of the Puritans and revival, I am indebted to Iain Murray, "The Puritans and Revival Christianity," *The Banner of Truth* 72 (September 1969): 9–19; J. I. Packer, "Puritanism as a Movement of Revival," *The Evangelical Quarterly* 52 (1980): 2–16; and Davies, *I Will Pour Out My Spirit*, 63–68. Packer's article can also be found in his *Quest for Godliness*, 35–48.

Emmanuel College, a hotbed of Puritan theology and piety, asked John to leave the college. Richard Rogers's wife convinced her husband to give the young man another opportunity. So the younger Rogers went up again to Cambridge only to prove the profligate once more, again selling his books and squandering the money obtained on his vices. His uncle would have washed his hands of him at that point, but yielding to the entreaties of his wife sent John up to Cambridge yet a third time. This time things proved to be quite different as a longsuffering God saved the young man and Richard later confessed, "I will never despair of a man for John Rogers' sake."

Most of Rogers's pastoral ministry after graduation was spent at what was then a Puritan stronghold in the parish of Dedham, Essex. He came to the Dedham church in 1605 and served there as a lecturer till his death thirty-one years later. A good number of Puritan leaders who had conscientious objections about aspects of the liturgy of the Church of England served as lecturers since this enabled them to preach, usually on a Sunday afternoon, outside of the framework of the typical Anglican service. According to the Puritan Sidrach Simpson, Rogers was an extraordinary preacher, both a "Boanerges, a Son of Thunder" (see Mark 3:17) and "a Barnabas, a Son of Consolation" (see Acts 4:36) through whose preaching "the stout hearts of many rebellious" sinners were humbled and led in submission to Christ.

The great Puritan theologian Thomas Goodwin (1600–1680) was present on one occasion when, during the course of a sermon, Rogers took the part of God, angry with His people for not prizing the Scriptures and not reading them. He threatened to take away the Bible from such an ungrateful people. Rogers then impersonated the people, falling to his knees in the pulpit and pleading with God not to give them a famine of hearing the Word of God. "Lord, whatsoever thou dost to us, take not thy Bible from us; kill our children, burn our houses, destroy our goods, only spare us thy Bible, take not away thy Bible." Goodwin recalled that the impact of the sermon was electrifying, as many of the people in the church were smitten in their consciences and reduced to copious weeping in repentance. Goodwin himself, not yet converted, was brought under deep conviction of sin.

When he came out of the church he was so overwhelmed with tears that he stood for fifteen minutes or so, leaning on the neck of his horse before he had the strength to mount.

The Puritans long prayed and labored for a national awakening that was Dedham writ large. Though these prayers and labors did not see an answer in their lifetime—such an awakening was to come in the eighteenth century—here at Dedham we clearly see an anticipation, an antepast, of the remarkable scenes of revival in the next century. Here is great encouragement not to give up praying if we do not see immediate fruit. Praying breath is never lost.

Kirk of Shotts, North Lanarkshire
Around the same time as this foretaste of revival in Dedham, a celebration of the Lord's Supper at Shotts near Glasgow on Sunday, June 20, 1630, was attended by such a rich sense of the presence of God that at the end of the services, instead of retiring to bed, folks continued together in prayer and devotion throughout the night. Evidently it was not the custom at that time to have a further service on the Monday following the Communion. Yet God had so presenced Himself with them that they were unable to part without further thanksgiving and praise. A Monday preaching service was therefore arranged and a young man called John Livingstone (1603–1672), chaplain to the Countess of Wigton, was persuaded to be the preacher.

He too had spent the previous night in prayer. Alone in the fields at eight or nine in the morning he was so overcome with a sense of his unworthiness (particularly as so many choice ministers and experienced Christians were present) that he thought he would slip away quietly. He had actually gone some way and was almost out of sight of the church when the words "Was I ever a barren wilderness or a land of darkness?" were so impressed upon his heart that he felt bound to return and preach. What was to ensue was a most remarkable demonstration of the power and the grace of God under the preaching of His Word.

Livingstone preached for about an hour and a half upon Ezekiel 36:25–26: "Then will I sprinkle clean water upon you, and ye shall be clean: from all your filthiness, and from all your idols, will I cleanse you. A new heart also will I give you, and a new spirit will I put within you: and I will take away the stony heart out of your flesh, and I will give you an heart of flesh." He was about to finish when a heavy shower of rain caused people in the churchyard to cover themselves hastily with their cloaks. This prompted the preacher to continue:

> If a few drops of rain so discompose you, how discomposed would you be, how full of horror and despair, if God should deal with you as you deserve? And God will deal thus with all the finally impenitent. God might justly rain fire and brimstone upon you, as he did upon Sodom and Gomorrah, and the other cities of the plain. But, for ever blessed be his name! the door of mercy still stands open for such as you are. The Son of God, by tabernacling in our nature, and obeying and suffering in it, is the only refuge and covert from the storm of divine wrath due to us for sin. His merits and mediation alone are the screen from that storm, and none but those who come to Christ just as they are, empty of everything, and take the offered mercy at his hand, will have the benefit of this shelter.[10]

In such a manner Livingstone continued preaching for a further hour, experiencing, in his own words, "such liberty and melting of heart, as I never had the like in public all my lifetime." Such a rich outpouring of the Spirit of God occurred that it was estimated close to five hundred individuals were converted in a single day.[11]

Kidderminster, Worcestershire

A third example of revival can be found at Kidderminster, where Richard Baxter (1615–1691) was the parish minister between the years 1641 and 1661.[12] When Baxter first arrived in the town the vast bulk of its inhabitants were, in Baxter's own words, "an ignorant, rude and revelling people…they had hardly ever had any lively serious preaching among them." Brawling was incessant and "the odious, swinish

---

10. Cited in "Revival Snapshots: Kirk of Shotts," *Evangelical Times* 31, no. 6 (June 1997): 16.

11. Michael J. Crawford, *Seasons of Grace: Colonial New England's Revival Tradition in Its British Context* (New York, NY: Oxford University Press, 1991), 24–25.

12. On this revival, see Evans, *Fire in the Thatch*, 43–56.

sin of tippling and drunkenness" was a civic vice.[13] But this was to change dramatically during the course of Baxter's ministry as the town, from being "a very ungodly place became a wonderful centre of piety and fervour."[14]

The face and soul of the entire community was revolutionized as a result of five things. First, there was Baxter's preaching, once on Sunday and once on Thursday. His preaching was nourished on "the strong meat of Calvinistic soteriology and Puritan practical writings" that had a realistic perspective on the nature of the human condition—it was fallen and sinful at the core—and a solid answer for it—trust in the death and resurrection of the Lord Jesus Christ. Then Baxter held a weekly pastor's forum for his flock for the purpose of theological discussion and prayer. In Baxter's words: "Every Thursday evening my neighbours met at my house, and there one of them repeated the sermon, and afterwards they proposed what doubts any of them had about the sermon, or any other case of conscience, and I resolved their doubts: and last of all I caused sometimes one, and sometimes another of them to pray."[15] Third, Baxter was assiduous in his distribution of hundreds of Bibles and good Christian books. And he gave away thousands of copies of his own books. Fourth, Baxter, like many of his fellow Puritans, was persuaded of the inestimable value of personally catechizing the households of his flock. In Baxter's case, this meant visiting around 800 families in the town on an annual basis. He and an assistant met with each family in the parish for an hour once a year. The assistant actually visited the families in their homes, while Baxter, due to ill-health, would receive them in his study.[16] Baxter

---

13. Cited in James I. Packer, introduction to *The Reformed Pastor*, by Richard Baxter, ed. William Brown (1862, Edinburgh: Banner of Truth, 1974), 11; and James I. Packer, "Great Pastors—V. Richard Baxter (1615–1691)," *Theology* 56 (1953): 175.

14. Percy Dearmer, selected and arranged, *Religious Pamphlets* (New York, NY: Henry Holt & Co.; London: Kegan Paul, Trench, Trübner & Co., 1898), 200.

15. Cited in Packer, introduction to *Reformed Pastor*, by Baxter, 13.

16. In 1671, when Baxter was 56, he recalled that from the age of fourteen "I have not been a year free from suffering, and since twenty two but few dayes, and since 1646 (which is about twenty five years), I have had but few hours free from pain (though through God's grace not intolerable)." N. H. Keeble, *Richard Baxter: Puritan Man of Letters* (Oxford: Clarendon Press, 1982), 11. He was, in J. I. Packer's memorable turn of phrase, "a veritable museum of

made it clear to the family that "this was to be a pastoral interview; notice was given to each family some weeks beforehand, and on the appointed day they were examined as to their knowledge of the Westminster Shorter Catechism and their spiritual well-being."[17] In Baxter's words:

> I have found by experience, that some ignorant persons, who have been so long unprofitable hearers, have got more knowledge and remorse of conscience in half an hour's close discourse, than they did from ten years' public preaching.
>
> I know that preaching the gospel publicly is the most excellent means, because we speak to many at once. But it is usually far more effectual to preach it privately to a particular sinner...for the plainest man that is, can scarcely speak plain enough in public for them to understand; but in private we may do it much more.... Besides we can better answer their objections, and engage them by promises before we leave them, which in public we cannot do. I conclude, therefore, that public preaching will not be sufficient: for though it may be an effectual means to convert many, yet not so many, as experience, and God's appointment of further means, may assure us. Long may you study and preach to little purpose, if you neglect this duty.
>
> [To one who objects that he does not have the time to personally visit each member of his flock]: What have we our time and strength for, but to lay them out for God? What is a candle made for, but to burn? Burned out and wasted we must be; and is it not fitter it should be in lighting men to heaven, and in working for God, than in living to the flesh?[18]

A final reason for the impact of the gospel in Kidderminster was Baxter's love for the people. He gave away much of his income to those in need. And until a properly qualified doctor came to the town Baxter served as a doctor for his parishioners, and that pro bono.[19]

The dramatic result of this ministry was a local revival. Here is Baxter's own account:

---

disease," *A Grief Sanctified: Passing Through Grief to Peace and Joy* (Ann Arbor, MI: Servant Publications, 1997), 43.

17. Packer, "Great Pastors," 178.
18. Baxter, *The Reformed Pastor*, 196–97, 218.
19. Packer, "Great Pastors," 176.

> The congregation was usually full, so that we were fain to build five galleries after my coming thither, the church itself being very capacious [it held up to a thousand people], and the most commodious and convenient that ever I was in. Our private meetings also were full. On the Lord's-days there was no disorder to be seen in the streets, but you might hear an hundred families singing psalms and repeating sermons as you passed through the streets. In a word, when I came thither first there was about one family in a street that worshipped God and called on his name, and when I came away there were some streets where there was not passed one family in the side of a street that did not do so, and that did not, by professing serious godliness, give us hope of their sincerity.[20]

The fruit of this ministry appears to have been genuine. It is fascinating to read a note that George Whitefield (1714–1770), the great evangelist of the eighteenth century, recorded in his diary on the last day of 1743 after a visit to Kidderminster: "I was greatly refreshed to find what a sweet savour of good Mr. Baxter's doctrine, works, and discipline remained to this day."[21]

Among those converted under Baxter's preaching at Kidderminster was Margaret Charlton (1636–1681). Like Baxter she came from Shropshire—she had in fact been raised only a few miles from where Baxter grew up, though in considerably wealthier circumstances. She came to live in Kidderminster with her godly mother, Mary Hanmer (d. 1661), who had been twice widowed and delighted in Baxter's pulpit ministry. Initially, Margaret had little liking for either Baxter or the people of the town. In Baxter's *A Breviate of the Life of Margaret, the Daughter of Francis Charlton...and Wife of Richard Baxter*—his account of their lives together, for Margaret became his wife—he tells us that she had a "great aversion to the poverty and strictness of the people" of the town. Frivolous and held in thrall at the time by the

---

20. *The Autobiography of Richard Baxter*, abr. J. M. Lloyd Thomas and ed. N. H. Keeble (London: J. M. Dent & Sons; Totowa, NJ: Rowman and Littlefield, 1974), 79. For an excellent study of Baxter's evangelism, see Timothy K. Beougher, "Richard Baxter and Puritan Evangelism," *Journal of the Academy for Evangelism in Theological Education* 7 (1991–1992): 82–94. See also the brief reflection by Gary E. Milley, "A Puritan Perspective on Preaching," *Resource* 2, no. 3 (January-February 1988): 16–17.

21. Cited in Packer, "Great Pastors," 175.

gaieties of this world, she was far more interested in "glittering herself in costly apparel."[22]

The Holy Spirit, though, was at work in her life. A series of sermons that Baxter preached on the doctrine of conversion, which eventually found their way into print as *A Treatise of Conversion* (1657), was, Baxter tells us, "received on her heart as the seal on the wax." Her spiritual transformation was swift and genuine. As she herself later wrote: "God hath…engaged me to himself, by taking me into his family, and planting me in his garden, and watering me with the dew from heaven…. I am thine, Lord, and not mine own…. Thou Lord that knowest all things, knowest that I have devoted my all to thee."[23]

Cote, Oxfordshire

At the close of the Puritan era there occurred a local awakening in Cote, Oxfordshire, a hamlet four miles or so due south of Witney and a mile north of the River Thames. The hamlet contains one of the finest extant examples of eighteenth-century Baptist Church architecture. The congregation that worshiped in this building had its roots in the preaching of a young fifteen- or sixteen-year-old by the name of Joseph Collett (1684–1741), who had come to a living faith as a small child. In his mid-teens Collett began to invite neighbors to worship in a large room in his parents' home at Cote around 1700.[24] The congregation soon filled the room, the entrance hall, and even overflowed into the garden. Joseph created an outdoor baptistery at the foot of his parents' garden in which to baptize converts.

Revival swept through the village and many of the families in Cote and the nearby villages of Bampton, Aston, and Standlake were converted. This remarkable move of God went on for the best part

---

22. Cited in John T. Wilkinson, *Richard Baxter and Margaret Charlton: A Puritan Love-Story* (London: Geogre Allen & Unwin, 1928), 70.

23. Cited in Wilkinson, *Richard Baxter and Margaret Charlton*, 78, 81.

24. On Collett, see Joseph Stennett, *The Happiness and Glory of Heaven, Considered as the House of God, and Prepared by His Son: A Sermon Occasioned by the Death of the Reverend Mr. Joseph Collet* (London: Aaron Ward, 1742), 65–75; John Stanley, *The Church in the Hop Garden: A Chatty Account of the Longworth-Coate Baptist Meeting* (London: Kingsgate Press, [1935]), 110–19.

of the next three years. In 1703, a wealthy individual in the village named John Williams gave land for a chapel to be built in 1704. The present building was erected on the site of this first chapel in 1756 during the ministry of the second pastor, Joseph Stennett (1717–1772), who preached Collett's funeral sermon. In the course of this sermon Stennett noted that central to Collett's usefulness as a minster of the gospel was the presence of the Holy Spirit. Collett "diligently sought by constant and fervent supplications" the gifts of the Spirit. "The rich grace of God" underlay his life of virtue and his firm commitment to the "good old principles of the Reformation."[25]

Praying for Revival

Glorious as these episodes of revival were, they were not the national awakening that the Puritans had longed to see. That longing can be seen, for instance, in a tract that was written by Abraham Cheare (1626–1668), the pastor of the Particular Baptist work in Plymouth, with the help of four other Baptist leaders—Henry Forty, Robert Steed, John Pendarves (1622–1656), and Thomas Glasse. Entitled *Sighs for Sion*, this tract essentially pled with the churches to which it was sent to pray for the outpouring of the Spirit that the authors deemed vital if they were to see their churches quickened and strengthened.[26] To stir up their readers to be fervent in prayer, Cheare and his coauthors cited examples of faithful praying from the Old Testament—men such as Nehemiah, Ezra, and Daniel.[27] In fact, the writers felt that God had already given the churches a foretaste of "this glorious blessing of the Spirit of grace and supplication"—a reference to Zechariah 12:10.[28] This foretaste gave Cheare and his fellow authors a longing for a greater blessing. They thus expressed their desire that they and their readers would live in such a way that

> the zeal of the Lord's house would eat us up, and love of it would crucify us more unto, and wean us from those interests of earth,

---

25. Stennett, *Happiness and Glory of Heaven*, 66.
26. Abraham Cheare et al., *Sighs for Sion* (London: Livewel Chapman, 1656), 10–11.
27. Cheare et al., *Sighs for Sion*, 12–13.
28. Cheare et al., *Sighs for Sion*, 15–16.

and men, whereupon we have been apt to lean, and whereunto we have been deeply and dangerously engaged: causing us also to wait to be with Jesus, which is best of all; and in the meantime to pant, and thirst incessantly, for that Holy Spirit of promise, that alone can present us with the ravishing glory of that expected day, and raise up our spirits to a sweet and suitable disposition, according to the will of God, to wait and act aright toward it.[29]

A similar "panting" for the outpouring of the Spirit can be seen in a letter written eighteen years later, in 1674, by the pastor-theologian John Owen (1616–1683), to Charles Fleetwood (ca. 1618–1692), one of Cromwell's sons-in-law. Owen began by expressing his fear that

> we shall die in the wilderness; yet ought we to labour and pray continually that the heavens would drop down from above, and the skies pour down righteousness—that the earth may open and bring forth salvation, and that righteousness may spring up together [see Ps. 85:10–11].... I beseech you to contend yet more earnestly than ever I have done, with God, with my own heart, with the church, to labour after spiritual revivals.[30]

Owen's fears were not unfounded: he would die without seeing any turning of the tide for the Nonconformists, and the spiritual state of England would continue to decline until the revivals of the mid-1730s. Owen's use of the term "revival" here—as a term for widespread spiritual awakening and significant numbers of conversions—is definitely one of the earliest usages of this term in this way in the history of Christian literature.[31] Given Owen's keen interest in the work of the Holy Spirit, however, it should not occasion any surprise that he would be among the first to so use the word "revival."

---

29. Cheare et al., *Sighs for Sion*, 19.

30. John Owen, Letter to Charles Fleetwood, July 8 [1674], in Peter Toon, ed., *The Correspondence of John Owen* (Cambridge: James Clarke, 1970), 159.

31. Danny Hyde, "John Owen on Revival," *The Aquila Report* (Wednesday, June 7, 2017; https://www.theaquilareport.com/john-owen-revival, accessed January 18, 2020). The bulk of this online article appeared in an earlier piece written by Hyde in 2011, which was cited by Kenneth J. Stewart, *Ten Myths About Calvinism: Recovering the Breadth of the Reformed Tradition* (Downer's Grove, IL: InterVarsity Press, 2011), 103n10.

Another early usage of this term occurs by Owen in a posthumously published tract entitled *Meditations and Discourses on the Glory of Christ, in His Person, Office, and Grace*. Here he is thinking of the need for personal revival, but what he says applies to the corporate sphere as well:

> Do any of us find decays in grace prevailing in us;—deadness, coldness, lukewarmness, a kind of spiritual stupidity and senselessness coming upon us? Do we find an unreadiness unto the exercise of grace in its proper season, and the vigorous acting of it in duties of communion with God? and would we have our souls recovered from these dangerous diseases? Let us assure ourselves there is no better way for our healing and deliverance, yea, no other way but this alone,—namely, the obtaining a fresh view of the glory of Christ by faith, and a steady abiding therein. Constant contemplation of Christ and his glory, putting forth its transforming power unto the revival of all grace, is the only relief in this case.[32]

Owen recommended "constant contemplation" of Christ and His glory as the pathway to personal spiritual revival. But why does such a focus bring about revival? Owen went on to explain:

> Some will say, that this [revival] must be effected by fresh supplies and renewed communications of the Holy Spirit. Unless he fall as dew and showers on our dry and barren hearts,—unless he cause our graces to spring, thrive, and bring forth fruit,—unless he revive and increase faith, love, and holiness in our souls,—our backslidings will not be healed, nor our spiritual state be recovered. Unto this end is he prayed for and promised in the Scripture. See Cant. 4:16; Isa. 44:3–4; Ezek. 36:26; Hos. 14:5–6.[33] And so it is. The immediate efficiency of the revival of our souls is from and by

---

32. John Owen, *Meditations and Discourses on the Glory of Christ, in His Person, Office, and Grace* in *The Works of John Owen*, ed. William H. Goold (1850–1855; London: Banner of Truth, 1965–1968), 1:395. I am indebted to Hyde, "John Owen on Revival," for this text and the next one.

33. Song 4:16: "Awake, O north wind; and come, thou south; blow upon my garden, that the spices thereof may flow out. Let my beloved come into his garden, and eat his pleasant fruits"; Isa. 44:3–4: "For I will pour water upon him that is thirsty, and floods upon the dry ground: I will pour my spirit upon thy seed, and my blessing upon thine offspring: And they shall spring up as among the grass, as willows by the water courses"; Ezek. 36:26: "A new heart also will I give you, and a new spirit will I put within you: and I will take away the stony heart out of your flesh, and I will give you an heart of flesh"; Hos. 14:5–6: "I will

the Holy Spirit. But the inquiry is, in what way, or by what means, we may obtain the supplies and communications of him unto this end. This the apostle declares in...[2 Cor. 3:18]: We, beholding the glory of Christ in a glass, "are changed into the same image from glory to glory, even by the Spirit of the Lord." It is in the exercise of faith on Christ...that the Holy Spirit puts forth his renewing, transforming power in and upon our souls. This, therefore, is that alone which will retrieve Christians from their present decays and deadness.[34]

The Holy Spirit is the only one who can revive God's people, corporately and personally, and He does so by means of focusing their thought upon the Lord Jesus's glory, life, cross-work, and ongoing ministry since His session at the Father's right hand.

Owen was not the only Puritan leader urging prayer for revival in the 1670s. Four years after Owen wrote this letter the Presbyterian John Howe (1630–1705) preached a series of sermons based on Ezekiel 39:29 in which he dealt with the subject of the outpouring of the Holy Spirit. In one of these sermons Howe told his audience:

> When the Spirit shall be poured forth plentifully I believe you will hear much other kind of sermons, or they will, who shall live to such a time, than you are wont to do now-a-days.... It is plain, too sadly plain, there is a great retraction of the Spirit of God even from us; we not know how to speak living sense [that is, felt reality] unto souls, how to get within you; our words die in our mouths, or drop and die between you and us. We even faint, when we speak; long experienced unsuccessfulness makes us despond; we speak not as persons that hope to prevail.... When such an effusion of the Spirit shall be as is here signified...[ministers] shall know how to speak to better purpose, with more compassion and sense, with more seriousness, with more authority and allurement, than we now find we can.[35]

---

be as the dew unto Israel: he shall grow as the lily, and cast forth his roots as Lebanon. His branches shall spread, and his beauty shall be as the olive tree, and his smell as Lebanon."

34. Owen, *Meditations and Discourses*, 1:395–96.

35. John Howe, *The Prosperous State of the Christian Interest Before the End of Time, By a Plentiful Effusion of the Holy Spirit: Sermon IV*, The Works of the Rev. John Howe, M. A. (New York, NY: John P. Haven, 1838), 1:575. For the explanation of "living sense" as "felt reality," see James I. Packer, *God In Our Midst: Seeking and Receiving Ongoing Revival* (Ann Arbor, MI: Servant Books, 1987), 33.

Behind the great evangelical revivals of the eighteenth century in the transatlantic world lie then the prayers and longings of countless Puritans and godly Christians going back at least to the seventeenth century. Such praying breath is never lost, but it is vital to recognize that man's timetable is not God's. The Puritans longed to see nationwide revival in their day, but it was not to be. Such days were to come, but not until the Puritan era was passed and the eighteenth century, sometimes called the Age of Reason, was well into its fourth decade.

CHAPTER 2

"God Is Doing Marvellous Things"
The British Need for and Experience of Revival in the Eighteenth Century

Secular historians remember the eighteenth century as the Age of Reason or the Enlightenment, when a number of key European intellectuals asserted the absolute independence and sovereignty of human reason. But it was also an age of remarkable spiritual awakening and revival, especially in the English-speaking world that spanned both sides of the Atlantic, revivals that completely reshaped many facets of the transatlantic British society. In the previous chapter, we closed with a quote from the Puritan leader John Howe in which he expressed his concern that Puritan pulpit of the 1670s lacked divine power. He saw this as a sign that the Spirit of God was no longer blessing the Puritan pulpit as He once had done. By the time that Howe died in 1705, there seemed to be no remedy in sight and the situation was even bleaker.

England and Wales in the Eighteenth Century

The final decades of the seventeenth century had seen a distinct decline in public manners and morals in England and Wales. Attestation of this fact is found in both public documents and private testimonies. Here is the witness of one Baptist author, Benjamin Keach (1640–1704), writing in 1701:

> Was ever sodomy so common in a Christian nation, or so notoriously and frequently committed, as by too palpable evidences it appears to be, in and about this city, notwithstanding the clear light of the gospel which shines therein, and the great pains taken to reform the abominable profaneness that abounds? Is it not a wonder the patience of God hath not consumed us in his wrath, before

this time? Was ever swearing, blasphemy, whoring, drunkenness, gluttony, self-love, and covetousness, at such a height, as at this time here?[1]

Despite the creation of gospel-centered pastorates and societies for moral reform such as the Society for the Reformation of Manners (founded in 1691), such public sins as homosexuality, profanity, sexual immorality, drunkenness, and gluttony were widespread. And the next three decades saw little improvement.

The moral tone of the nation was set in many ways by its monarchs and leading politicians. George I (1660–1727), who reigned from 1714 to 1727, was primarily interested in food, horses, and women. He divorced his wife when he was thirty-four and thereafter consorted with a series of mistresses.[2] Sir Robert Walpole (1676–1745), prime minister from 1722 to 1742, lived in undisguised adultery with his mistress, Molly Skerrett (1702–1738), whom he married after his wife died.[3] As English historian J. H. Plumb has noted of aristocratic circles in the early eighteenth century, the women "hardly bothered with the pretense of virtue, and the possession of lovers and mistresses was regarded as a commonplace, a matter for gossip but not reproach."[4] Not surprisingly other segments of society simply followed suit. Pornographic literature, for instance, multiplied almost unchecked, newspapers advertised such things as the services of gigolos and cures for venereal disease, and one could purchase guidebooks to the numerous brothels in London.[5]

Social conditions were equally bleak. While many of the rich indulged themselves and all of their whims, the lot of the ordinary man and woman was quite different. For a variety of economic causes the towns of England mushroomed in the eighteenth century. The population of London, the capital, more than doubled. By the end of the century, it contained over a million people and was the largest

---

1. Benjamin Keach, *Gospel Mysteries Unveiled* (1701, London: L. I. Higham, 1817), 3:310.
2. J. H. Plumb, *The First Four Georges* (London: B. T. Batsford Ltd., 1956), 39–42.
3. J. H. Plumb, *Sir Robert Walpole* (Clifton, NJ: Augustus M. Kelley, 1973), 2:114.
4. Plumb, *Sir Robert Walpole*, 2:114.
5. Roy Porter, *English Society in the Eighteenth Century* (Harmondsworth, Middlesex: Penguin Books Ltd., 1982), 279.

city in the western world.⁶ Many men and women came to these cities from rural poverty, hoping to find a decent living. But adequate housing could not keep up with the demand and those who most needed the shelter lacked sufficient funds to purchase it.⁷ Consequently, houses were desperately overcrowded. In a large industrial center like Manchester, for example, ten people living in a room was common. Such rooms were often without furniture and lacked even beds. The occupants would sleep close together on wood shavings for warmth. Disease was rampant and unchecked: smallpox, typhus, typhoid, and dysentery made death a very familiar figure.⁸

From such a dismal existence, many sought escape in drink. Beer had always been a central part of English life. But in the eighteenth century many turned to something far more potent: gin. By mid-century, the consumption of poorly distilled and often virtually poisonous gin was eleven million gallons a year. Some idea of the debilitation wrought by this plague of alcoholism may be grasped in terms of a simple item of record. In one area of London, for instance, comprising two thousand houses or so, 506 were gin shops. One contemporary novelist, Henry Fielding (1707-1754), estimated that in London one hundred thousand people drank gin as their principal means of sustenance. Even if Fielding was exaggerating, this is still horrifying.⁹ The sort of suffering that such consumption of gin brought in its wake is well illustrated by a news item from 1748 which reads as follows: "At a christening at Beddington in Surrey the nurse was so intoxicated that after she had undressed the child, instead of laying it in the cradle she put it behind a large fire, which burnt it to death in a few minutes."¹⁰

---

6. J. H. Plumb, *England in the Eighteenth Century* (Harmondsworth, Middlesex: Penguin Books Ltd., 1963), 144.

7. David Lyle Jeffrey, ed., introduction to *A Burning and a Shining Light: English Spirituality in the Age of Wesley* (Grand Rapids: Eerdmans, 1987), 9.

8. Plumb, *England in the Eighteenth Century*, 12.

9. Jeffrey, introduction to *Burning and a Shining Light*, 9.

10. Cited in Porter, *English Society*, 35.

When we turn to the religious situation of early eighteenth-century England and Wales we find churches basically unable to cope with the increasingly dire moral and social situation. The dominant religious grouping was the Church of England, which was the established church of the land. But it was largely helpless when it came to dealing with social and moral problems. First of all, at this time the Church of England was primarily a rural-based denomination. Despite the large-scale population shift toward industrial, urban centers, the Church of England stayed in the country. Moreover, in the words of Plumb, many of the leading figures in the Church, its bishops, were "first and foremost politicians, and politicians are rarely men of the spirit. There is a worldliness…about eighteenth-century [bishops] which no amount of apologetics can conceal. The[ir] clerical duties…were done only as political duties allowed."[11]

The worldliness of these bishops showed in other ways as well. Jonathan Trelawny, Bishop of Winchester, used to "excuse himself for his much swearing by saying he swore as a baronet, and not as a bishop"![12] Such bishops had neither the time nor the interest to promote church reform. Of course, the decadence of church leadership was by no means absolute. But the net effect of worldly bishops was to squash effective reform.

The clergy under these bishops also failed to see the seriousness of the situation. Far too many of those who were well-to-do devoted themselves to anything but their ministries: philosophy, biology, agriculture, chemistry, literature, law, politics, fox hunting, drinking—all claimed the attention of these ministers. Many of the ministers, though, barely eked out a living. Few of them—wealthy or poor—preached anything but dry, unaffecting sermons. In a diary kept by a shopkeeper named Thomas Turner (1729–1793) from East Krathly, Sussex, such preaching was insightfully criticized as an

> idle lazy way of preaching, which many of our clergy are got into, seeming rather to make self-interest the motive for the exercising

---

11. Plumb, *England in the Eighteenth Century*, 43.

12. Cited in J. Wesley Bready, *England Before and After Wesley: The Evangelical Revival and Social Reform* (London: Hodder and Stoughton Ltd., 1938), 50.

their profession than the eternal happiness and salvation of men's souls. To which if we add the intolerable degree of pride and covetousness predominant in too many of our clergy, we need not wonder at our degeneracy from the strict piety with which our forefathers worshipped God in the first ages of Christianity.[13]

The situation was little different in Wales. Church attendance during the early eighteenth century was infrequent and, when it did occur, it was often accompanied by irreverence.[14] When the Anglican minister Ellis Wynne o Lasynys (1671–1734) published his Welsh prose classic *Gweledigaetheu y bardd cwsc* (*Visions of the Sleeping Bard*) in 1703, he described his experience of Anglican worship thus:

> There I saw some whispering, some laughing; others eyeing young maidens; yet others surveying the dress of their neighbours from head to toe; some fighting and quarreling about privileged positions, some asleep, others diligent in their devotion, and some of these even were hypocrites.[15]

Diocesan records for Wales are replete with clergymen being censured for immorality, drunkenness, vile speech, and a crass neglect of their duties.[16]

Part of the reason for this spiritual ineffectiveness of the ministers of the Church of England in England and Wales is the fact that in the year 1662 around two thousand ministers of the Church of England, the most spiritually minded group of the established Church at the time, had been expelled from her ranks for refusing to conform completely to the rites and practices of the Church of England. These men and women, known to history as the Puritans, had sought unsuccessfully for close to a hundred years to bring reform and renewal to the Church of England. Eventually these ministers and their congregations were forced out to join three fledgling denominations: the English Presbyterians, the Independents of Congregationalists,

---

13. Thomas Turner, entry for January 20, 1758, in *The Diary of Thomas Turner, 1754–1765*, ed. David Vaisey (Oxford; New York, NY: Oxford University Press, 1984), 131.
14. Eifion Evans, *Daniel Rowland and the Great Evangelical Awakening in Wales* (Edinburgh: Banner of Truth, 1985), 12.
15. Cited in Evans, *Daniel Rowland*, 12.
16. Cited in Evans, *Daniel Rowland*, 13.

and the Particular Baptists, also known as the Calvinistic Baptists. These three groups, along with an Arminian body, the General Baptists, became known as the "Dissenters" or "Nonconformists." Little wonder then that the Church of England found herself at a distinct spiritual disadvantage when it came to leading the nation in moral and spiritual reform in the early eighteenth century. Many of the most spiritual men and women in England were now marginalized as Dissenters.

Of the three Dissenting denominations, it was especially the Congregationalists and the Particular Baptists who stayed true to Christian orthodoxy during the eighteenth century. But, for reasons which will be given in a later chapter, far too many of these Dissenters—especially the Particular Baptists—were stagnant and not reaching out to the unsaved with the gospel. The spiritual situation in which early eighteenth-century Dissenters thus found themselves is well described by two Congregationalist ministers in 1737, Isaac Watts (1674–1748), the father of the English hymn, and John Guyse (1680–1761). "There has been a great and just complaint for many years," they wrote, "that the work of conversion goes on very slowly, that the Spirit of God in his saving influences is much withdrawn from the ministrations of his word, and there are few that receive the report of the gospel, with any eminent success upon their hearts." They were thus constrained to pray, "Return, O Lord, and visit thy churches, and revive thine own work in the midst of us."[17]

Revival in Wales: Its Preparation

Now, it is an amazing fact that the revival for which Isaac Watts and John Guyse prayed did not originate in England among the Dissenters—the heirs of Puritanism, the leading evangelical movement of the seventeenth century—but within that body which had actually persecuted the Puritans, namely, the Church of England. From our perspective, this fact can only be seen as a display of God's sovereignty!

---

17. Isaac Watts and John Guyse, preface to *A Narrative of a Surprising Work of God*, by Edwards, in *Jonathan Edwards on Revival* (Edinburgh: Banner of Truth, 1965), 2–3.

The first flames of revival in the British Isles were visible in Wales. During the days of the English Republic in the 1640s and the 1650s, special attention had been paid to Wales by Puritan leaders such as the Congregationalists Walter Cradock (ca. 1610–1659) and Morgan Llwyd (1619–1659), the open-membership Baptist preacher Vavasor Powell (1617–1670), and John Miles (1621–1683), the father of the Baptist movement in Wales.[18] But after the Restoration of Charles II (1630–1685) many areas of Wales lapsed into moral and doctrinal decline. Heightening this state of affairs was the fact that Welsh was the dominant language of the country and there was little by way of Christian literature in Welsh.

One key Welshman, though, who was deeply moved by the spiritual ignorance rampant in Wales before the revivals and who was greatly used of God to prepare the way for these revivals was the Anglican clergyman, Griffith Jones (1683/1684–1761), who has been well described as "the Morning Star" of the eighteenth-century awakenings,[19] and whom one author has gone so far to call "the greatest Welshman of the eighteenth century."[20] Born in Carmarthenshire, Griffith Jones was christened on May 1, 1684, two months after the death of his father, John ap Griffith. His early years were spent keeping sheep, though a longing for education was eventually realized when he went to study at Carmarthen Grammar School. Converted at a young age, he was encouraged by a local minister to seek his vocation within the Church of England. He was ordained in September 1708, and, because of the spiritual power attending his preaching he was soon speaking to large crowds in southern Wales. By the time that he came to the final parish that he was to serve, in Llandowror, Carmarthenshire, in 1717, he was widely known as a remarkable preacher of the gospel. It is noteworthy that not only in message and

---

18. D. Densil Morgan, "Continuity, Novelty and Evangelicalism in Wales c. 1640–1850" in Michael A. G. Haykin and Kenneth J. Stewart, ed., *The Emergence of Evangelicalism: Exploring Historical Continuities* (Nottingham: InterVarsity Press, 2008), 90–92.

19. Christopher J. Tokeley, "Griffith Jones, 'Morning Star' of the Evangelical Revival in Wales," *In Writing: The Magazine of the Evangelical Library* 114 (Spring 2008): 26–31.

20. Geraint Jenkins, "'An Old and Much Honoured Soldier': Griffith Jones, Llanddowror," *The Welsh History Review* 11 (1983): 449. See also Evans, *Fire in the Thatch*, 57–74.

method [field-preaching], but also in the opposition he aroused, Jones anticipated George Whitefield and the Wesley brothers, John (1703–1791) and Charles (1707–1788).

Even more remarkable than his career as an evangelist was his work for religious education. He saw that no kind of renewal of Christianity could take place amid an ignorant and untutored population. In order to raise the literacy level, he developed a catechetical class, which met on Sunday evenings. This developed into the Circulating Welsh Charity Schools. In the beginning, he found that of the sixty to eighty children who came into his schools, not more than three or four could say the Lord's Prayer. The schools began in the winter of 1731–1732; they expanded to the point that, by his death in 1761, there were almost 3,325 schools which, by a conservative estimate, taught two hundred thousand to read, at a time when the population of Wales was between four hundred thousand and five hundred thousand.[21] One other significant aspect of Griffith Jones's ministry was his reliance on the Holy Spirit. This is clear from the following text that he wrote in 1733:

> I wish I had more of the unction of this Holy Spirit to carry me through the work of my day and assist me to live in a closer communion with God. It has sometimes refreshed my soul to consider that among all the precious promises in the Holy Scriptures, there is not one more full, and worded in stronger terms of assurance, than that of the heavenly Father giving the Holy Spirit to them that ask Him, Luke 11:13. And this should put us upon asking in faith, which can never fail to succeed.[22]

Another key preparatory figure of the Welsh revival was a Particular Baptist by the name of Enoch Francis (1688–1740), who ministered within twenty miles of Griffith Jones's parish. Wherever he went, vast crowds would assemble to hear him preach free salvation through the amazing love of Christ. It was said that he rarely preached without tears streaming down his face, which was something of an exception

---

21. It is noteworthy that "the areas in which the Methodist societies had established themselves by about 1740 were exactly those regions of the south where the schools were." Philip Jenkins, *A History of Modern Wales 1536–1990* (London: Longman, 1992), 156.

22. Cited in Evans, *Daniel Rowland*, 34–35.

among Welsh Baptists of that time.[23] But the two key figures in the Welsh revival belonged to Church of England: Howell Harris (1714–1773) and Daniel Rowland (1711–1790).

Howell Harris and Daniel Rowland

Griffith Jones was the morning-star of the revival in Wales and Daniel Rowland was possibly the most prominent preacher in it, but it was the conversion of Howell Harris in 1735 which directly initiated the Welsh Revival.[24] On Palm Sunday of that year Howell Harris, a schoolmaster who was taken up with "dice playing, drinking, gossiping and love-making,"[25] attended morning worship at Talgarth Parish Church. The vicar, Pryce Davies (d. 1761), gave an exhortation before the Lord's Supper: "If you are not fit to come to the Lord's Supper… you are not fit to live; you are not fit to die."[26] For eight weeks Harris was in spiritual turmoil till at last, on Pentecost Sunday at the Lord's Table, he received assurance that his sins were forgiven.

In 1736 Harris was introduced to Griffith Jones, and over the next fifteen years he spent a good amount of time at Llandowror, where Jones was rector.[27] Harris flayed his body to preach the gospel. At first, he tried to combine school teaching in the day with preaching in the evening, making do with two hours' sleep at night or none at all. But at the end of 1737 the school managers issued an ultimatum: "Either stop preaching or leave school." He left and till 1749 devoted his life to itinerant evangelism. For example, over one period of thirty-three days in 1747 he wrote in his journal: "I traveled about 600 miles… and came home at two in the morning last Sunday after traveling last week about 250 miles."[28]

---

23. Evans, *Daniel Rowland*, 15.
24. Michael R. Watts, *The Dissenters: From the Reformation to the French Revolution* (Oxford: Clarendon Press, 1978), 396.
25. A. Skevington Wood, *The Inextinguishable Blaze: Spiritual Renewal and Advance in the Eighteenth Century* (Grand Rapids: Eerdmans, 1960), 48.
26. Cited in Wood, *Inextinguishable Blaze*, 49.
27. Geoffrey F. Nuttall, *Howell Harris, 1714–1773: The Last Enthusiast* (Cardiff: University of Wales Press, 1965).
28. Watts, *Dissenters*, 397.

During this time, Harris had no definite income. And he often went without adequate meals and more than once had to sell his books to buy food. Concerning his journeys, he said: "I travel the least expensive…often eating a cake or an apple in order to be sparing [that is, to avoid dining at an inn]."[29] But the experience of God's power through Harris's preaching impelled him to continue and under his ministry, hundreds were soundly converted and organized into religious societies.[30] Like Griffith Jones, Harris was convinced of the vital importance of having the Holy Spirit's power and anointing. As he once asked, "What is the Bible but a dead letter to us till we do experience the work of the Holy Spirit in us?"[31]

By 1747, though, Harris was physically exhausted and really needed a complete rest. But in his zeal he labored on. On top of his physical exertion, while preaching in Bala, North Wales, in 1748, he was suddenly attacked and received, he later said, "a blow on the head with violence enough to slit my head in two."[32] Although he said that he had not been affected by the blow, there was possibly some temporary damage, for his actions over the next few years became quite odd and he began to put forward some strange ideas.

He asserted that it was God the Father who died on the cross and that "there is no God but Jesus Christ." He threatened to part company with any who disagreed with him on this score.[33] He bought tickets in a lottery in the hope of winning money that he said he would use to support an orphanage that Whitefield had established in Georgia.[34] He also created confusion in the revival by claiming that his ministry was superior to that of Rowland.

---

29. Arnold A. Dallimore, *George Whitefield: The Life and Times of the Great Evangelist of the Eighteenth-Century Revival* (1979, Westchester, IL: Cornerstone Books, 1980), 2:295.

30. Nuttall, *Howell Harris*, 16–17.

31. Cited in R. Tudur Jones, "The Evangelical Revival in Wales: A Study in Spirituality," in *An Introduction to Celtic Christianity*, ed. James P. Mackey (Edinburgh: T&T Clark, 1989), 249.

32. Cited in Dallimore, *George Whitefield*, 2:298.

33. Dallimore, *George Whitefield*, 2:299.

34. Dallimore, *George Whitefield*, 2:297.

Possibly the most foolish of his actions in this period of time was Harris's admittance to his home of a Mrs. Sidney Griffith (d. 1752), or "Madam Griffith," as she was wont to be called, the wife of a boorish, drunken squire. She had fled her husband and taken refuge with Harris and his wife. She was, it seems, "a woman of some strength of personality, mental ability and personal attractiveness."[35] In time, Harris came to believe that she had been possessed the apostolic gift of prophecy and discernment of spirits.[36] And since Harris's wife refused to accompany him on his evangelistic tours, Madam Griffith went in her stead.[37] There was no evidence that the association was immoral, but it was highly indiscreet and harmful.[38] When Whitefield learned of Harris's association with Mrs. Griffith he travelled especially to Wales to order her out of the Harris home.[39] She refused to leave and actually accompanied Harris to London in 1751, where Harris tried to preach for Whitefield. The latter lovingly refused to allow him to preach, whereupon Harris became severely critical of Whitefield and made a number of irresponsible remarks about him. Thankfully, for the sake of the revival and Harris's ministry, Mrs. Griffith died in 1752.

Harris returned home from London to Wales a very sick man. In fact, for the next two years, from 1751 to 1753, he was frequently confined to his bed with what he described as an "unbearable headache" and "excruciating pains in my head."[40] This man, who had been a spiritual father to thousands, found himself all but deserted. But after about two years his health began to return. He built additions to his home at Treveca to create a religious community for a Christian commune of sorts. And in the 1760s, after Harris had confessed his former indiscretions and apologized for them, he was restored once again to a place of prominence in the revival. Harris's experience

---

35. Dallimore, *George Whitefield*, 2:298.
36. Dallimore, *George Whitefield*, 2:299.
37. Watts, *Dissenters*, 419.
38. Nuttall, *Howell Harris*, 51–52.
39. Dallimore, *George Whitefield*, 2:300.
40. Dallimore, *George Whitefield*, 2:300.

reveals that times of revival can also be times of great spiritual danger even for leaders like him.

The other key figure in the revival was Daniel Rowland, an Anglican curate who came from a family of clergymen. He was converted in the same year as Harris. The instrument of conversion was none other than Griffith Jones, who had come to preach in Rowland's parish church. According to one account, when Jones came into the pulpit, he noticed the skeptical look on the young curate's face. Jones thus paused to pray, not only for Rowland's salvation but also that Rowland might become the instrument of turning many to Christ. Jones's prayer of faith was more than abundantly answered. In that very service, Rowland was brought under a profound conviction of sin and subsequently soundly converted.[41]

Christmas Evans (1766–1838), himself a gifted preacher, once said of his fellow Welshman, "Rowland was a star of the greatest magnitude…and perhaps there has not been his like in Wales since the days of the apostles."[42] Yet he was less well known than Harris because his papers and writings were totally in Welsh and many of these were lost shortly after his death in 1790. Rowland was a careful preacher. His library contained a number of works by the early Fathers as well as much solid theology from his own day. Though Rowland would only take into the pulpit a small piece of paper with the outline of his sermon, behind it there was much preparation. In his early days Rowland preached for three to four hours. As he grew more skilled as a preacher, though, three-quarters of an hour was sufficient.[43]

What is very significant is that Rowland, like Griffith Jones, was aware that the source of his power in ministry was the Holy Spirit. As Rowland once noted, "If God does not pluck us, as brands out of the burning fire, by his free grace, and remove by his Spirit the veil of darkness and ignorance from our minds, none can be saved."[44] One

---

41. Wood, *Inextinguishable Blaze*, 45–46; Evans, *Daniel Rowland*, 33–34.
42. Cited in Evans, *Daniel Rowland*, 1–2.
43. Alan Luff, "250 Years of the Welsh Revival," *The Expository Times* 97, no. 12 (1986): 366.
44. Evans, *Daniel Rowland*, 374.

Sunday morning a friend found Rowland still lying in bed and urged him to make haste to get dressed and ready for the pulpit. "I am not quite ready," he replied. "I have nothing from the Lord to say to the people! I was looking up all last night and had no sleep!" Rowland was not merely referring to the matter of sermon preparation. He also had in mind the Holy Spirit's preparation of the preacher's heart.[45] Typical of those converted under Rowland was Thomas Charles (1755–1814), who would himself become a great preacher. Charles was converted in 1773 at Llangeitho. He later described his experience thus:

> The change a blind man who received his sight experiences doth not exceed the change I at that time experienced in my mind…I had such a view of Christ as our high priest, of his love, compassion, power, and all-sufficiency as filled my mind with astonishment—with joy unspeakable and full of glory.[46]

Scotland and Revival

Another Celtic land deeply impacted by the revival was Scotland. As was the case of the national church in England and Wales, the spirituality of the national Presbyterian Church of Scotland in the first three decades of the eighteenth century was at low ebb. What has come to be called Moderatism was on the rise in this era. Those who adhered to this perspective distrusted confessional statements like the Westminster Confession. They did not openly oppose them, but rather hoped that by not mentioning them, they would be conveniently forgotten. As one writer advised in an unpublished, anonymous text: "Do not contradict the received doctrines [of the Westminster Confession] in your sermons. You will defeat them better by letting them fall into desuetude."[47] Moderates clearly rejected their forebears' conviction that adherence to Christian orthodoxy was essential for being a Christian. Rather, they conceived of the Christian faith as largely a matter of morality and public virtue. In their hands, Christianity

---

45. Evans, *Daniel Rowland*, 373–74.
46. Jenkins, *History of Modern Wales*, 160.
47. Cited in Arthur Fawcett, *The Cambuslang Revival: The Scottish Evangelical Revival of the Eighteenth Century* (London: Banner of Truth, 1971), 27. "Desuetude" means "discontinuance from use or exercise."

became "the cult of Good Manners, of first and last, polish. Presbyterianism had to be shown as a religion fit for gentlemen."[48]

Local awakenings were sporadically occurring during the 1720s and 1730s. Typical of these revivals was one that took place in 1739 at Nigg on the Easter Ross Peninsula, due north of Inverness, where forty were converted during this one year.[49] A far more extensive work began at Cambuslang in the Lowlands a few years later in 1742 under the preaching of William McCulloch (1691–1771), who was the minister of Cambuslang, at that time a rural parish a few miles to the southeast of Glasgow. McCulloch was far from being an accomplished speaker. In the jargon then current, he was a yill- or ale-minister, a term that was used of ministers whose preaching was so dry that when their turn came to preach at the large outdoor Communion gatherings then held once a year by the Scottish churches, many of the audience would leave to quench their thirst from nearby ale barrels provided for refreshment.[50] Yet it was under McCulloch's preaching in mid-February, 1742, that, according to the English Nonconformist Philip Doddridge (1702–1751), around one hundred and thirty people, most of whom had sat under McCulloch's preaching for a number of years, "were awakened on a sudden to attend to it, as if it had been a new revelation brought down from heaven, and attested by as astonishing miracles as ever were wrought by Peter or Paul."[51]

In July of the same year the preeminent English evangelist George Whitefield (1714–1770), whose ministry we shall look at in the next chapter, arrived at Cambuslang. He was soon preaching to huge, receptive audiences. In August, for instance, we are told that some thirty thousand attended an outdoor Communion service where Whitefield preached a number of sermons over the course of a three-day weekend. Alexander Webster, a minister from Edinburgh, wrote of some of the remarkable happenings of that weekend:

---

48. Fawcett, *Cambuslang Revival*, 2.
49. Wood, *Inextinguishable Blaze*, 117–18; Davies, *I Will Pour Out My Spirit*, 87.
50. Crawford, *Seasons of Grace*, 160.
51. Philip Doddridge, *Some Remarkable Passages in the Life of the Honourable Col. James Gardiner*, sec. 22, *The Works of The Rev. P. Doddridge, D.D.* (Leeds, 1803), 4:88.

> During the time of divine worship, solemn, profound reverence overspread every countenance. They hear as for eternity.... Thousands are melted into tears. Many cry out in the bitterness of their soul. Some...from the stoutest man to the tenderest child, shake and tremble and a few fall down as dead. Nor does this happen only when men of warm address alarm them with the terrors of the law, but when the most deliberate preacher speaks of redeeming love.[52]

Well do the following words of Jonathan Edwards (1703–1758), in a letter that he wrote to William McCulloch in May of 1743, sum up this revival at Cambuslang: "We live in a day wherein God is doing marvellous things: in that respect, we are distinguished from former generations."[53]

A number of the Scottish ministers involved in the leadership of this revival—men such as William McCulloch, John McLaurin (1693–1754) of the Ramshorn Church in northwest Glasgow, James Robe (1688–1753) of Kilsyth, and John Erskine (1721–1803) of Kirkintilloch—would spend much energy in the years that followed promoting revival, and in doing so link arms with like-minded brothers and sisters across the Atlantic in America. As we shall see, these transatlantic links, especially with Jonathan Edwards, would prove to be of great significance in the history of revival. Equally important was regular correspondence between John Erskine and a couple of young Baptists in the final decades of the eighteenth century. Again, we shall see how this correspondence was instrumental in both revival and the initiation of key elements in the globalization of evangelical Christianity.

---

52. Cited in Dallimore, *George Whitefield*, 2:128. For further details and discussion of this revival, see especially Fawcett, *Cambuslang Revival*; Crawford, *Seasons of Grace*.

53. Jonathan Edwards, Letter to William McCulloch, May 12, 1743, in Sereno E. Dwight, "Memoirs of Jonathan Edwards, A. M." in *The Works of Jonathan Edwards* (1834, Edinburgh: Banner of Truth, 1987), 1:lxxii.

CHAPTER 3

"Come to This Life-Giving Stream"
George Whitefield and His Ministry in a Time of Revival

In 1835 Francis Alexander Cox (1783–1853) and James Hoby (1788–1871), two prominent English Baptists who were visiting fellow Baptists in the United States, made a side trip to Newburyport, Massachusetts to view the tomb of George Whitefield. The "grand itinerant," as he was then known, had died on September 30, 1770, at the home of Jonathan Parsons (1705–1776), pastor of the town's First Presbyterian Church, also known as Old South. He had been interred two days later in a vault below what is now the center aisle of this church, where, along with the coffins of Parsons and another pastor of the church, Joseph Prince (d. 1791), his remains were on display all through the nineteenth century. In fact, it was not until 1932 that the coffin in which Whitefield's remains lay was covered over with a slate slab.[1]

Cox and Hoby later recalled descending with some difficulty into the subterraneous vault where Whitefield was buried. As they did so, they remembered that "deep expectant emotions thrilled our bosoms." They sat on the two other coffins in the vault and watched as the upper half of the lid of Whitefield's coffin was opened on its hinges "to reveal the skeleton secrets of the narrow prison–house." They "contemplated and handled the skull," while they "thought of his devoted life, his blessed death, his high and happy destiny" and "whispered [their] adorations of the grace that formed him both for earth and heaven."[2] What makes this scene even more *outré* is that the

---

1. G. Norris Foster, compiled, *First Presbyterian Church (Old South), Newburyport, Massachusetts: Historical Notes and Dates* (n.p., n.d.), 1.

2. F. A. Cox and James Hoby, *The Baptists in America: A Narrative of the Deputation from the Baptist Union in England to The United States and Canada* (London: T. Ward &

skeletal remains that Cox and Hoby viewed were not intact. The main bone of Whitefield's right arm had been stolen some years earlier by another Englishman. It was not until either the late 1830s or even the 1840s that the thief's conscience brought him to the point of sending the bone back across the Atlantic in a small wooden box![3]

These accounts are a potent reminder of the fact that of all the great preachers raised up in the transatlantic evangelical Revival none gripped the public mind and imagination more than George Whitefield. During his lifetime, the Congregationalist Joseph Williams (1692–1755), a merchant from Kidderminster with a keen interest in spiritual renewal, rightly termed him the "Father" of those seeking to advance the revival.[4] Henry St. John, Viscount Bolingbroke (1678–1751), who "professed himself a deist," was forced to exclaim, after hearing Whitefield preach: "the most extraordinary man of our times, the most commanding eloquence, unquenchable zeal, unquestionable piety."[5] On the other side of the Atlantic Benjamin Colman (1673–1747) and William Cooper (1694–1743) viewed Whitefield as "the wonder of the age" and were convinced that "no man more employs the pens, and fills up the conversation of people, than he does at this day."[6] Shortly after the evangelist's death Augustus Montague Toplady (1740–1778), author of the famous hymn "Rock of Ages, Cleft for Me,"

Co., 1836), 421–22. For other similar accounts, see L. Tyerman, *The Life of the Rev. George Whitefield* (New York, NY: Anson D. F. Randolph & Co., 1877), 2:602–3, 607.

3. Foster, *First Presbyterian Church (Old South)*, 1, 8. Tyerman gives the date for the bone's return as 1837 (*George Whitefield*, 2:606). Robert Philip, Whitefield's nineteenth-century biographer, knew the thief and urged him to return it. The thief sought to show Philip the bone in 1835, but the latter refused to gaze upon it. See Philip's *The Life and Times of the Reverend George Whitefield, M.A.* (London: George Virtue, 1838), 550–51.

4. "Charles Wesley in 1739 by Joseph Williams of Kidderminster," introduction to Geoffrey F. Nuttall, *Proceedings of the Wesley Historical Society* 42, no. 6 (December 1980): 182.

5. Cited in Willard Connely, *The True Chesterfield: Manners—Women—Education* (London: Cassell and Co. Ltd., 1939), 179.

6. Benjamin Colman and William Cooper, "To the Reader," preface to *The Character, Preaching, etc. of the Reverend Mr. George Whitefield, Impartially Represented and Supported*, by Joseph Smith, in George Whitefield, *Fifteen Sermons Preached on Various Important Subjects* (Glasgow: J. & W. Shaw, 1792), 5–6.

remembered him as "the apostle of the English empire."[7] And looking back from the following century, John Foster (1770–1843), the Baptist essayist, was sure that with "the doubtful exception of Wickliffe, no man probably ever excited in this island [that is, the British Isles] so profound, and extended, and prolonged a sensation in the public mind, by personal addresses to the understanding and conscience, on the subject of religion."[8]

"A Ray of Divine Life": The Pathway to Conversion[9]

George Whitefield was the youngest son of Thomas Whitefield (1681–1716), the proprietor of the Bell Inn, at the time the finest hotel in Gloucester. George's father died when he was but two and so he was raised by his mother Elizabeth (ca. 1681–1751). His school record was unremarkable, save for a noticeable talent for acting. As he later said, "During the time of my being at school, I was very fond of reading plays, and have kept from school for days together to prepare myself for acting them."[10] For a while during his teen years, when his older brother Richard took over the running of the inn, he worked as one of the servants. But his mother longed for something better for her son. Her persistence and the kindness of friends enabled him in November

---

7. Augustus M. Toplady, "A Concise Character of the Late Rev. Mr. Whitefield," *The Works of Augustus Toplady, B.A.* (London: J. Chidley, 1837), 494.

8. John Foster, "George Whitefield: A Critical Essay" in *George Whitefield's Journals (1737–1741)* (1905, Gainesville, FL: Scholars' Facsimiles & Reprints, 1969), 15.

9. The best biographical study of Whitefield is Dallimore's two-volume *George Whitefield: The Life and Times of the Great Evangelist of the Eighteenth-Century Revival*. Dallimore has also written a one-volume account of Whitefield's life: *George Whitefield: Evangelist of the 18th-Century Revival* (London: The Wakeman Trust, 1990). For another excellent biography, see Thomas S. Kidd, *George Whitefield: America's Spiritual Founding Father* (New Haven; London: Yale University Press, 2014). See also Michael A. G. Haykin, *George Whitefield* (Darlington, England: EP Books, 2014). For two studies that are more critical and controversial in nature, see Harry S. Stout, *The Divine Dramatist: George Whitefield and the Rise of Modern Evangelicalism* (Grand Rapids: Eerdmans, 1991) and Frank Lambert, *"Pedlar in Divinity": George Whitefield and the Transatlantic Revivals, 1737–1770* (Princeton, NJ: Princeton University Press, 1994). For an insightful critique of Stout, see Eric Carlsson, "Book Reviews: Harry S. Stout, *The Divine Dramatist: George Whitefield and the Rise of Modern Evangelicalism,*" *Trinity Journal*, ns 14, no. 2 (Fall 1993): 238–47.

10. Cited in Jerome Dean Mahaffey, *The Accidental Revolutionary: George Whitefield and the Creation of America* (Waco, TX: Baylor University Press, 2011), 3.

1732 to enter Pembroke College, Oxford University. It was here in the following summer that he first met John Wesley (1703–1791) and his younger brother Charles (1707–1788), who were regularly meeting with a group of men known to history as "the Holy Club." This was a company of ten or so men who were ardently trying to live religious lives in an extremely dissolute age.

Whitefield, like-minded and longing for spiritual companionship ever since coming up to Oxford, joined them. He engaged in numerous religious exercises such as fasting, praying regularly, attending public worship, and seeking to abstain from what were deemed worldly pleasures. Systematic reading of Puritan and Pietist devotional literature also occupied much of Whitefield's time.[11] Despite the evident zeal he brought to these religious activities he had no sense of peace with God or that God was satisfied with what he was doing. Although he did not know it at the time, he was treading a pathway similar to the one that Martin Luther (1483–1546) had taken over two hundred years earlier. And just as Luther's conversion was the spark that lit the fires of the Reformation, so Whitefield's conversion would be central to kindling the blaze of the eighteenth-century Evangelical Revival.

Conversion came in the spring of 1735 after Charles Wesley had given him a copy of *The Life of God in the Soul of Man* (1677) by Henry Scougal (1650–1678), a former professor of divinity at Aberdeen.[12] This book was a frontal challenge to Whitefield's ardent endeavor to create a righteous life that would merit God's favor. As Whitefield recalled it many years later in a sermon that he preached in 1769:

---

11. On the role that reading played in his conversion and his subsequent growth as a Christian, see Lambert, *"Pedlar in Divinity,"* 17–21. It is interesting that it was Christian literature, not the spoken word, that played the vital role in the conversion of Whitefield, although he is best remembered as a preacher (Lambert, *"Pedlar in Divinity,"* 18). On Whitefield's later reading, see the helpful article by John Lewis Gilmore, "Preparation: the Power of Whitefield's Ministry," *Christianity Today* 24, no. 5 (March 7, 1980): 22–24.

12. For a modern edition of this work, see Henry Scougal, *The Life of God in the Soul of Man* (Fearn, Ross-shire: Christian Focus Publications, 1996).

I must bear testimony to my old friend Mr. Charles Wesley, he put a book into my hands, called, *The Life of God in the Soul of Man*, whereby God shewed me, that I must be born again, or be damned. I know the place: it may be superstitious, perhaps, but whenever I go to Oxford, I cannot help running to that place where Jesus Christ first revealed himself to me, and gave me the new birth. As a good writer [Scougal] says, a man may go to church, say his prayers, receive the Sacrament, and yet, my brethren, not be a Christian. How did my heart rise, how did my heart shudder, like a poor man that is afraid to look into his account–books, lest he should find himself a bankrupt: yet shall I burn that book, shall I throw it down, shall I put it by, or shall I search into it? I did [search it], and, holding the book in my hand, thus addressed the God of heaven and earth: Lord, if I am not a Christian, if I am not a real one, for Jesus Christ's sake, shew me what Christianity is, that I may not be damned at last. I read a little further, and the cheat was discovered; O, says the author, they that know any thing of religion know it is a vital union with the Son of God, Christ formed in the heart; O what a ray of divine life did then break in upon my poor soul.[13]

Awakened by this book to his need for the new birth, Whitefield passionately struggled to find salvation along the pathway of extreme asceticism but to no avail. Finally, when he had come to an end of his resources as a human being, God enabled him, in his words, "to lay hold on His dear Son by a living faith, and, by giving me the Spirit of adoption, to seal me, as I humbly hope, even to the day of everlasting redemption." And, he went on, "oh! With what joy—joy unspeakable—even joy that was full of, and big with glory, was my soul filled."[14]

"The Open Bracing Air": The Life of a Preacher

Always the avid reader, it was Whitefield's prayerful perusal of the Puritan biblical commentaries of William Burkitt (1650–1703) and Matthew Henry (1662–1714) a few months after his conversion that led to his becoming convinced of "free grace and the necessity of

---

13. George Whitefield, "All Men's Place," in his *Sermons on Important Subjects* (London: Thomas Tegg, 1833), 755.

14. George Whitefield, *Journals* (London: Banner of Truth, 1960), 58.

being justified in His [that is, God's] sight by *faith only*."[15] Following his ordination as deacon in the Church of England the following year these Reformation doctrines came to occupy a central place in his preaching arsenal.[16] There is, for instance, an account of Whitefield's preaching drawn up by an unknown French contemporary. Dated August 1739, this observer states that Whitefield preaches "continually about inner regeneration, the new birth in Jesus Christ, the movement of the Spirit, justification by faith through grace [*justification par la foy de grace*], the life of the Spirit."[17]

The following year Joseph Smith, a Congregationalist minister from Charleston, South Carolina, defended Whitefield against various attacks in his *The Character, Preaching, etc. of the Reverend Mr. George Whitefield, Impartially Represented and Supported*.[18] In the section dealing with the doctrinal content of Whitefield's sermons, Smith lists four "primitive, protestant, puritanic" doctrines that Whitefield regularly heralded in his preaching in America—original sin, "justification by faith alone," the new birth, and "inward feelings of the Spirit."[19] Smith recalled the way in which Whitefield "earnestly contended for our justification as the free gift of God, by faith alone in the blood of Christ, an article of faith delivered to the saints of old… telling us plainly, and with the clearest distinction, that a man was justified these three ways; meritoriously by Christ, instrumentally by faith alone, declaratively by good works."[20]

Whitefield's preaching on the new birth, though, was not at all well received by the Anglican clergy in England and churches began to be

---

15. Whitefield, *Journals*, 62. On his reading of Matthew Henry, see David Crump, "The Preaching of George Whitefield and His Use of Matthew Henry's *Commentary*," *Crux* 25, no. 3 (September 1989): 19–28; and Barry C. Davis, "George Whitefield's Doctrine of Scripture in Light of 18th Century Biblical Criticism," *Methodist History* 36, no.1 (October 1997): 20.

16. Dallimore, *George Whitefield*, 1:124–28.

17. Jeremy Black, "The Origins of Methodism: An Unpublished Early French Account," *Enlightenment and Dissent* 6 (1987): 116.

18. For this tract, originally a sermon, see Whitefield, *Sermons on Important Subjects*, 791–99. For its historical context, see Dallimore, *George Whitefield*, 1:511–14.

19. Whitefield, *Sermons on Important Subjects*, 792–95.

20. Whitefield, *Sermons on Important Subjects*, 793.

barred to him. Whitefield, however, was not to be deterred. On Saturday, February 17, 1739, he made the decision to take to the open air and preach to a group of colliers in Kingswood, a coalmining district on the outskirts of Bristol. These men with their families lived in squalor and utter degradation, squandering their lives in drink, violence, and sex. With no church nearby, they were quite ignorant of Christianity and its leading tenets. It was a key turning point in not only his life but also in the history of evangelicalism.[21] The concern that has gripped evangelicals in the last two hundred years to bring the gospel message directly to ordinary people has some of its most significant roots here in Whitefield's venturing out to preach in the open air.

From this point on Whitefield would relish and delight in his calling as an open-air preacher. He would preach in fields and foundries, in ships, cemeteries, and pubs, atop horses and even coffins, from stone walls and balconies, staircases and windmills.[22] For instance, referring to this calling in a letter dated December 14, 1768, he wrote, "I love the open bracing air." And the following year he could state: "It is good to go into the high–ways and hedges. Field-preaching, field-preaching for ever!"[23]

---

21. For much of the nineteenth and twentieth centuries, Whitefield's innovative role in this regard was forgotten. The publication of Dallimore's two-volume *George Whitefield* has certainly gone far in redressing this amnesia. Yet even today good historians can forget this fact and see John Wesley as the real innovator. See, for example, Mark Noll, *Turning Points: Decisive Moments in the History of Christianity* (Grand Rapids: Baker Books, 1997), 221–44, where Noll mentions Whitefield as an innovator in open-air preaching (*Turning Points*, 223, 238–39), but then emphasizes that it was Wesley's decision to preach in the fields two months after Whitefield that was the critical turning point in the history of evangelicalism. Gordon Wakefield, though, in his essay "John and Charles Wesley: A Tale of Two Brothers" has it right when he says that it was Whitefield "and not the Wesleys who may be said to have begun the Evangelical Revival in 1737" in Geoffrey Rowell, ed., *The English Religious Tradition and the Genius of Anglicanism* (Nashville, TN: Abingdon Press, 1992), 172.

22. In light of his own itinerant ministry, it is interesting to read the following remarks on Jesus's ministry. Christ, he wrote in 1756, "taught all that were willing to hear, on a mount, in a ship, or by the sea-side." See Letter MCXVII to the Bishop of B—, February 2, 1756, in *The Works of the Reverend George Whitefield, M.A.* (London: Edward and Charles Dilly, 1771), 3:157.

23. *Works of the Reverend George Whitefield*, 3:379, 387. It is noteworthy that Whitefield never lost elements of his West-country accent. He would pronounce "Christ" as "Chroist," for example; see J. I. Packer, "The Spirit with the Word: The Reformational

It should also be noted that Whitefield never confined his witnessing about Christ to preaching occasions. He took every opportunity to share his faith. "God forbid," he once remarked, "I should travel with anybody a quarter of an hour without speaking of Christ to them."[24] On another occasion, during his sixth preaching tour of America, he happened to stay with a wealthy, though worldly, family in Southold on Long Island. The family discovered after the evangelist had left their home that he had written with a diamond on one of the windowpanes in the bedroom where he had slept, "One thing is needful"![25]

At that first open-air service in February 1739 there were two hundred or so. Within about six weeks, Whitefield was preaching numerous times a week to crowds sometimes numbering in the thousands![26] Whitefield's description of his ministry at this time is a classic one. To visualize the scene at the Kingswood collieries, we need to picture the green countryside, the piles of coal, the squalid huts, and the deep semicircle of unwashed faces as we read his words:

> Having no righteousness of their own to renounce, they were glad to hear of a Jesus who was a friend of publicans, and came not to call the righteous, but sinners to repentance. The first discovery of their being affected was to see the white gutters made by their tears which plentifully fell down their black cheeks, as they came out of their coal pits. Hundreds and hundreds of them were soon brought under deep convictions, which, as the event proved, happily ended in a sound and thorough conversion. The change was visible to all, though numbers chose to impute it to anything, rather than the finger of God.[27]

Revivalism of George Whitefield" in *The Bible, the Reformation and the Church: Essays in Honour of James Atkinson*, ed. W. P. Stephens (Sheffield: Sheffield Academic Press, 1995), 170. And his fellow evangelical John Wesley (1703–1791) could mention Whitefield's "little improprieties…of…language" (Packer, "Spirit with the Word," 171, n. 20).

24. George Whitefield, "Jacob's Ladder," in his *Sermons on Important Subjects* (London: Thomas Tegg, 1833), 774.

25. Iain Murray, introduction to *Journals*, by Whitefield, 13.

26. George Whitefield, Letter to Daniel Abbot, February 24, 1739 (Graham C. G. Thomas, "George Whitefield and Friends: The Correspondence of Some Early Methodists," *The National Library of Wales Journal* 27 [1991]: 83).

27. Cited in Dallimore, *George Whitefield*, 1:263–64.

Here is another description from this same period of time, when others besides the miners of Bristol were flocking to hear Whitefield preach:

> As…I had just begun to be an extempore preacher, it often occasioned many inward conflicts. Sometimes, when twenty thousand people were before me, I had not, in my own apprehension, a word to say either to God or them. But I never was totally deserted, and frequently…so assisted, that I knew by happy experience what our Lord meant by saying, "Out of his belly shall flow rivers of living water" (John 7:38). The open firmament above me, the prospect of the adjacent fields, with the sight of thousands and thousands, some in coaches, some on horseback, and some in the trees, and at times all affected and drenched in tears together, to which sometimes was added the solemnity of the approaching evening, was almost too much for, and quite overcame me.[28]

Revival had come to England! And to that revival, and its confluent streams in Wales, Scotland, and British North America no man contributed more than Whitefield. Over the thirty-four years between his conversion and death in 1770 in Newburyport, Massachusetts, it has been calculated that he preached around eighteen thousand sermons.[29] Actually, if one includes all of the talks that he gave, he probably spoke about a thousand times a year during his ministry.[30] Moreover, while some of his talks were delivered to small groups, many of his sermons were delivered to massive congregations that numbered ten thousand or so, some to audiences possibly as large as fifteen thousand.[31]

In addition to his preaching throughout the length and breadth of England, he regularly itinerated throughout Wales, visited Ireland twice, and journeyed fourteen times to Scotland. He crossed the Atlantic thirteen times, stopping once in Bermuda for eleven weeks, and preached in virtually every major town on the Atlantic seaboard.[32] What is so remarkable about all of this is Whitefield lived at

---

28. Cited in Dallimore, *George Whitefield*, 1:268.
29. Toplady, "Anecdotes, Incidents and Historic Passages" in his *Works*, 495.
30. Dallimore, *George Whitefield*, 2:522.
31. For the numbers, see Dallimore, *George Whitefield*, 1:263, 267, 295–96; 2:522–23.
32. He was in America during 1738, 1739–1741, 1744–1748, 1751–1752, 1754–1755, 1763–1765, and 1769–1770.

a time when travel to a town but twenty miles away was a significant undertaking. In journeying to Scotland and to America he was going to what many perceived as the fringes of transatlantic British society and culture. And yet some of God's richest blessings on his ministry were in these very regions.[33] For example, Harry Stout, commenting on Whitefield's impact on America, writes:

> So pervasive was Whitefield's impact in America that he can justly be styled America's first cultural hero. Before Whitefield, there was no unifying intercolonial person or event. Indeed, before Whitefield, it is doubtful any name other than royalty was known equally from Boston to Charleston. But by 1750 virtually every American loved and admired Whitefield and saw him as their champion.[34]

Whitefield's ministry—insisting, as it did, on the vital necessity of conversion and the work of the Holy Spirit in the heart—was not without its critics, many of whom castigated him for what they regarded as fanaticism. And it needs to be admitted that in his early ministry Whitefield did make some unguarded statements and adopted certain attitudes that helped fuel this opposition. On his second preaching tour of America, for instance, Whitefield appears to have maintained that assurance belonged to the essence of saving faith and that a mature Christian could discern the marks of conversion in another individual. To his credit, Whitefield would later admit his injudiciousness and that he had been far "too rash and hasty" in his speech and published writings. "Wild-fire has been mixed with it," he wrote in 1748, "and I find that I frequently wrote and spoke in my own spirit, when I thought I was writing and speaking by the assistance of the Spirit of God."[35] Despite these faults—basically overcome by his early thirties—multitudes of Whitefield's hearers found his preaching "moving, earnest, winning, melting" and rooted in a doctrinal framework that was "plainly that of the Reformers."[36]

---

33. Whitefield had a great admiration for many American ministers. As he said in his final sermon in England, "no place under heaven produces greater divines than New England" ("The Good Shepherd" in *Sermons on Important Subjects*, 782).

34. Harry Stout, "Heavenly Comet," *Christian History* 38 (1993): 13–14.

35. George Whitefield, Letter DCXL to the Rev. Mr. S—, June 24, 1748 (*Works*, 2:144).

36. These are the words of Thomas Prince (1687–1758), a New England pastor and

"An Insatiable Thirst of Travelling":
Taking the Word over Land and Sea

In the early years of the revival Whitefield's itinerant, open-air preaching was also often paraded as evidence of his "enthusiasm" or fanaticism. Part of Whitefield's response to this criticism was to go back to the example of the apostle Paul as found in the book of Acts. "Was he not filled," he asked his opponents, "with a holy restless impatience and insatiable thirst of travelling, and undertaking dangerous voyages for the conversion of infidels?"[37] Here Whitefield reveals the spiritual passion that spurred his own incessant traveling over land and sea: the longing to see sinners embrace Christ as Lord and Savior and find their deepest spiritual thirst and hunger satisfied in Christ alone.

Criticism of the wide-ranging nature of his ministry also came from such ardent evangelicals as Ebenezer Erskine (1680–1754) and his younger brother Ralph (1685–1752), founders of the Secession Church in Scotland.[38] This body of churches had seceded from the national church in the 1730s over the issue of whether or not the people of a congregation had the right to refuse a minister chosen for them by the Presbytery or heritors (that is, landowners who possessed hereditary rights to property within a parish). The Erskines had invited Whitefield to preach solely in their churches. But Whitefield refused to be pinned down to a few locales and insisted on preaching wherever he was given a pulpit in Scotland.[39] He told the Erskines that he was "more and more determined to go out into the highways and

---

historian. They are cited by John Gillies, *Historical Collections of the Accounts of Revival* (1845; Edinburgh: Banner of Truth, 1981), 350, 351.

37. George Whitefield, *Some Remarks on a Pamphlet, entitled, The Enthusiasm of Methodists and Papists compar'd* (London, 1749), 26.

38. On the Erskines, see Alan P. F. Sell, "'The Message of the Erskines for Today," *The Evangelical Quarterly* 60 (1988): 299–316; Joel Beeke, "The Ministry of the Erskines" (two papers presented at the Twenty-first Annual Banner of Truth Ministers' Conference, Grantham, Pennsylvania, May 26–27, 1999). For another perspective on Whitefield's relationship with the Erskines, see also Kenneth B. E. Roxburgh, *Thomas Gillespie and the Origins of the Relief Church in 18th Century Scotland* (Bern: Peter Lang, 1999), 31–39.

39. George Whitefield, Letter 33 to John Willison, August 17, 1742, in *Letters of George Whitefield for the period 1734–1742* (Edinburgh: Banner of Truth, 1976), 514–15.

hedges; and that if the Pope himself would lend me his pulpit, I would gladly proclaim the righteousness of Jesus Christ therein."[40]

That Whitefield failed to understand the concern of the Erskines for the reformation of the church is evident in the sad disagreement between them. Yet his reply well reveals his passion for the salvation of the lost wherever they might be. As he told the Scottish Lord Rae a few days after this discussion with the Erskines, the "full desire" of his soul was to "see the kingdom of God come with power." He was, he went on, "determined to seek after and know nothing else. For besides this, all other things are but dung and dross."[41] Still in Scotland two months later, the same spiritual desire continued to deeply grip him. "I want a thousand tongues to set off the Redeemer's praise," he told the Earl of Leven and Melville.[42] Five years later, while the surrounding scenery is different—he is on his third preaching tour of America—this passion burned as bright as ever. "Oh that I was a flame of pure & holy fire, & had [a] thousand lives to spend in the dear Redeemer's service," he told Joshua Gee (1698–1748), for the "sight of so many perishing souls every day affects me much, & makes me long to go if possible from pole to pole, to proclaim redeeming love."[43] "Had I a thousand souls and bodies," he noted on another occasion, "they should be all itinerants for Jesus Christ."[44]

Nothing gave Whitefield greater joy than to report to his friends that God was blessing his preaching. "The word runs and is glorified," a line from Paul's second letter to the Thessalonians (2 Thess. 3:1), and Jesus's statement to His disciples that the fields were "white already to harvest" (John 4:35) were frequent refrains in his correspondence. Writing from Pennsylvania in May 1746, Whitefield informed a correspondent in Gloucestershire, England, that Christ "gives me full

---

40. George Whitefield, Letter CCCXXXIX to Thomas Noble, August 8, 1741 (*Works*, 1:308).

41. George Whitefield, Letter CCCXLIII, August 11, 1741 (*Works*, 1:311).

42. George Whitefield, Letter CCCLVI, October 2, 1741 (*Works*, 1:323).

43. George Whitefield, Letter to Revd. Mr. Gee, June 21, 1746, in John W. Christie, "Newly Discovered Letters of George Whitefield, 1745–46, III," *Journal of The Presbyterian Historical Society* 32 (1954): 261.

44. George Whitefield, Letter [DCCCCLXXXV] to Mr. G—, July 21, 1753 (*Works*, 3:24).

employ on this side the water, & causes his word to run & be glorified.... Everywhere the fields are white ready unto harvest. I am just now going to tell lost sinners that there is yet room for them in the side of Jesus."[45] Upon hearing of the marriage of one of his nephews in 1756 Whitefield observed, "Alas, what a changing world do we live in! Blessed be God for an unchangeable Christ! Amidst all, this is my comfort, his word runs and is glorified."[46] Christ "vouchsafes daily (O amazing love) to own my feeble labours," he told a friend in 1757. Then he added: "The word runs and is glorified."[47] Or writing to a fellow minister in Scotland only a couple of years before his death: "In London the word runs and is glorified, and in Edinburgh, I trust, the prospect is promising. The fields are white ready unto harvest."[48]

"Streams of Mercy, Never Ceasing": Four Conversions

Another vantage point from which to view Whitefield's ministry of the Word is to look at the impact of his preaching on various individuals. Let us consider four, three of them writers of verse.[49] First, there is Thomas Olivers (1725–1799), the Welsh Methodist who was later closely associated with the Wesleys and the author of the well-known hymn "The God of Abraham Praise."[50] Notorious for his addiction to foul swearing and in his own words, "one of the most profligate and abandoned young men living," Olivers went to hear Whitefield preach in Bristol in 1748. The evangelist's text was Zechariah 3:2: "Is not this

---

45. George Whitefield, Letter to Mr. Adams, May 15, 1746 (Christie, "Newly Discovered Letters II," 163).
46. George Whitefield, Letter MCXLII to Mrs. C—, June 21, 1756 (*Works*, 3:185).
47. George Whitefield, Letter MCLXIV to the Reverend Mr. B—, March 10, 1757 (*Works*, 3:202).
48. George Whitefield, Letter MCCCLXXXIX to the Reverend Mr. T—, July 4, 1768 (*Works*, 3:371).
49. For a study of this subject, see the insightful paper by D. Bruce Hindmarsh, "'My Chains Fell Off, My Heart Was Free': Early Methodist Conversion Narrative in England," *Church History* 68 (1999): 910–29.
50. The following account of Olivers's conversion comes from Thomas Jackson, ed., *Wesleys's Veterans: Lives of Early Methodist Preachers Told by Themselves* (1837–1838, London: Robert Culley, 1909), 1:205–6.

a brand plucked out of the fire?" When Whitefield began his sermon Olivers said,

> I was certainly a dreadful enemy to God and to all that is good... but by the time it was ended I was become a new creature. For, in the first place, I was deeply convinced of the great goodness of God towards me all my life, particularly in that he had given his Son to die for me. I had also a far clearer view of all my sins, particularly my base ingratitude towards him. These discoveries quite broke my heart, and caused showers of tears to trickle down my cheeks. I was likewise filled with an utter abhorrence of my evil ways, and was much ashamed that ever I had walked in them. And as my heart was thus turned from all evil, so it was powerfully inclined to all that is good. It is not easy to express what strong desires I had for God and his service, and what resolutions I had to seek and serve him in future; in consequence of which I broke off all my evil practices, and forsook all my wicked and foolish companions without delay, and gave myself up to God and his service with my whole heart.

The first Sunday after his conversion Olivers was up early to attend the 6:00 a.m. worship service at Bristol Cathedral. During it, he later said, "I felt as I had done with earth, and was praising God! No words can set forth the joy, the rapture, the awe, and reverence I felt."

Another hymnwriter who made a profession of faith as a result of hearing Whitefield preach was Robert Robinson (1735–1790).[51]

---

51. On the life of Robinson, see especially Graham W. Hughes, *With Freedom Fired: The Story of Robert Robinson, Cambridge Nonconformist* (London: Carey Kingsgate Press, 1955); L. G. Champion, "Robert Robinson: A Pastor In Cambridge," *The Baptist Quarterly* 31 (1985–1986): 241–46; Len Addicott, introduction to *Church Book: St Andrew's Street Baptist Church, Cambridge 1720–1832*, by Addicott, L. G. Champion, and K. A. C. Parsons ([London]: Baptist Historical Society, 1991), viii–xviii; Karen Smith, "The Liberty Not to Be a Christian: Robert Robinson (1735–1790) of Cambridge and Freedom of Conscience" in Marc A. Jolley and John D. Pierce, ed., *Distinctively Baptist: Essays on Baptist History. A Festschrift in honor of Walter B. Shurden* (Macon, GA: Mercer University Press, 2005), 151–70.

I am well aware that Robinson's theological convictions in his final days have been the subject of considerable discussion and disagreement. There are reports that he questioned the doctrine of the Trinity, for instance. On the other hand, however, one of his oldest friends, Coxe Feary (1759–1822), pastor of the Particular Baptist work in Bluntisham, Huntingdonshire (see below in this chapter for a brief account of Feary's conversion and ministry), recorded a conversation that he had with Robinson but a month before the latter's death in 1790. Robinson affirmed that when it came to the doctrine of the Trinity he was neither a Unitarian nor an Arian. "My soul rests its whole hope of salvation," he

When Robinson first went to hear Whitefield preach his motivation in going was an odd one to say the least. On Sunday morning, May 24, 1752, he and some friends were out looking for some amusement when they came across an aged woman who claimed to be a fortune teller. After they had gotten her thoroughly drunk on what was probably cheap gin, they proceeded to have her tell their fortunes. When it came to Robinson, the woman predicted that he would live to see his children, grandchildren, and even great-grandchildren growing up around him.

Now, what had started as something of a lark was taken quite seriously by Robinson as he made his way home later that day. When he was alone, he thought that if he were indeed to live to such a ripe age, he would probably end up being a burden to his family. There were in those days no such things as social security or welfare. What then could he do? Well, he thought, one way for those who are older to make themselves liked by their grandchildren is to have a good stock of stories to draw upon to entertain them. He thus determined there and then to fill his mind with knowledge and "everything that is rare and wonderful," which, when he was old, would stand him in good stead and cause him, so he reasoned, to "be respected rather than neglected."[52]

As his first acquisition, he decided to experience one of Whitefield's sermons. He went to hear him, though, as he later told the famous preacher, with feelings of pity for "the folly of the preacher" and "the infatuation of the hearers"—those "poor deluded Methodists"— and of abhorrence for Whitefield's doctrine.[53] Whitefield was preaching that evening at the Tabernacle, his meetinghouse in Moorfields,

---

solemnly told Feary, "on the atonement of Jesus Christ, my Lord and my God," Joseph Belcher, "Note" in his ed., *The Complete Works of the Rev. Andrew Fuller*, rev. Joseph Belcher, 3rd London ed. (1845, Harrisonburg, VA: Sprinkle Publications, 1988), 2:223–24.

52. [Andrew Fuller], "Anecdote," *The Evangelical Magazine*, 2 (1794): 72–73. Fuller had received this account of Robinson's conversion from Robinson himself. The story was written under the name of "Gaius," the pen name that Fuller regularly used.

53. Robert Robinson, Letter to George Whitefield, May 10, 1758, in William Robinson, ed., *Select Works of the Rev. Robert Robinson, of Cambridge* (London: J. Heaton & Son, 1861), 166–67.

London. His text was Matthew 3:7, John the Baptist's stern rebuke of the Pharisees and the Sadducees, "O generation of vipers, who hath warned you to flee from the wrath to come?" When, according to Robinson,

> Mr. Whitefield described the Saducean character; this did not touch me, I thought myself as good a Christian as any man in England. From this he went to that of the Pharisees. He described their exterior decency, but observed that the poison of the viper rankled in their hearts. This rather shook me. At length, in the course of his sermon, he abruptly broke off; paused for a few moments; then burst into a flood of tears; lifted up his hands and eyes, and exclaimed, "O my hearers! *The wrath's to come, the wrath's to come!*" These words sunk into my heart, like lead in the waters. I wept, and when the sermon was ended, retired alone. For days and weeks I could think of little else. Those awful words would follow me, wherever I went, "*The wrath's to come, the wrath's to come*"![54]

For over three years Robinson was haunted by these words and Whitefield's sermon. He regularly attended the preaching at the Tabernacle and found himself "cut down for sin" and "groaning for deliverance." Eventually on Tuesday, December 10, 1755, "after having tasted the pains of rebirth," Robinson "found full and free forgiveness through the precious blood of Jesus Christ."[55] Robinson eventually went on to pastor St. Andrew's Street Baptist Church in Cambridge, where he became one of the best colloquial preachers of the day. About two and a half years after his profession of faith Robinson wrote a hymn long treasured by God's people: "Come, Thou Fount of Every Blessing." It appears to have been written to commemorate what God did for him when He saved him.

> Come, Thou Fount of every blessing,
> Tune my heart to sing Thy grace;
> Streams of mercy, never ceasing,
> Call for songs of loudest praise.
> Teach me some melodious sonnet,
> Sung by flaming tongues above;

---

54. [Fuller,] "Anecdote," 73.
55. Robinson, Letter to George Whitefield (Robinson, ed., *Select Works*, 167); William Robinson, "Memoir [of Robert Robinson]" in his ed., *Select Works*, xv–xvi, footnote.

Praise the mount; I'm fixed upon it,
Mount of God's unchanging love.[56]

Then, listen to Phillis Wheatley (1753–1784), brought as a slave to America from her native Gambia or Senegal when she was seven. Sold to a merchant by the name of John Wheatley, he named her Phillis after the slave ship in which she was transported to America. Encouraged in her poetry by John and his wife Susanna, she eventually became the first published African American poetess. In an elegy for Whitefield, written after his death, she recalls the impact of his preaching on her when she heard Whitefield probably in Boston's Old South Church:

> He pray'd that grace in every heart might dwell,
> He long'd to see *America* excel;
> He charg'd its youth to let the grace divine
> Should with full lustre in their conduct shine;
> That Saviour, which his soul did first receive,
> The greatest gift that ev'n a God can give,
> He freely offer'd to the num'rous throng,
> That on his lips with list'ning pleasure hung.
>
> Take him, ye wretched, for your only good,
> Take him ye starving sinners, for your food;
> Ye thirsty, come to this life-giving stream,
> Ye preachers, take him for your joyful theme;
> Take him my dear *Americans*, he said,
> Be your complaints in his kind bosom laid:
> Take him, ye *Africans*, he longs for you,
> *Impartial Saviour* is his title due:
> Wash'd in the fountain of redeeming blood,
> You shall be sons, and kings, and priests to God.[57]

Wheatley has eloquently captured the way that Whitefield pled with his hearers and that he was able to speak to all of the various types of people who came to hear him preach.

---

56. On this hymn see the remarks of Erik Routley, *I'll Praise My Maker: A Study of the Hymns of Certain Authors Who Stand in or near the Tradition of English Calvinism 1700–1850* (London: Independent Press Ltd., 1951), 260–62.

57. Phillis Wheatley, "On the Death of the Rev. Mr. George Whitefield," lines 20–37, in her *Complete Writings*, ed. Vincent Carretta (New York; London: Penguin Group, 2001), 15–16.

In recent days, Whitefield's endorsement of the social order, especially regarding slavery, has been the subject of much concern, and rightly so.[58] Whitefield was directly responsible for the introduction of slaves into the colony of Georgia—he believed he needed them to labor on property that he had acquired for an orphanage—and so Whitefield became a slave owner. Whitefield believed a type of benevolent Christian slave owning was feasible. In the words of the American scholar, Stephen J. Stein, which he penned nearly fifty years ago, Whitefield went so far as to help "erect the theological defense for slavery and thus participated in a tragic chapter of the nation's experience."[59] After his death other evangelicals, such as John Wesley, held to an entirely different opinion on slavery. By 1772, Wesley publicly abominated the slave trade as "that execrable sum of all villainies."[60] Wesley published a pamphlet against slavery in 1774 entitled *Thoughts upon Slavery*.[61] This important pamphlet argued that slavery deprived the Africans of their "natural right" to liberty. In language that borrowed from western liberal thought, Wesley asserted: "Liberty is the right of every human creature, as soon as he breathes the vital air; and no human law can deprive him of that right which he derives from the law of nature."[62] Moreover, Wesley appealed to the solidarity between white Europeans and black Africans based on a common Creator. The Africans were fellow human beings and not a whit inferior to Europeans. To the end of his life Wesley fiercely denounced, in print and from the pulpit, the practice of slavery. Following his lead, the Wesleyan Methodists in the British Empire, the fastest-growing denominational body in the English-speaking world in the late eighteenth and early

---

58. See, for example, Dallimore, *George Whitefield*, 2:520–21; Kidd, *George Whitefield*, 188–203, 261–62; Kidd, "George Whitefield's Troubled Relationship to Race and Slavery," *The Christian Century*, January 6, 2015, http://www.christiancentury.org/blogs/archive/2015-01/george-whitefield-s-troubled-relationship-race-and-slavery.

59. Stephen J. Stein, "George Whitefield on Slavery: Some New Evidence," *Church History*, 42 (1973): 256.

60. *The Journal of the Rev. John Wesley A.M.*, ed. Nehemiah Curnock (London: Epworth Press, 1914), 5:445–46.

61. John Wesley, "Thoughts upon Slavery" in *The Works of John Wesley*, 3rd ed. (1872, Peabody, MA: Hendrickson, 1984), 11:59–79.

62. Wesley, "Thoughts upon Slavery," 11:79.

nineteenth centuries, brought their strength to bear as a vocal, highly organized pressure group against the whole institution of slavery and were influential in causing its demise.[63] If Whitefield had lived another decade or so, would he have come to see the error of his thinking about slavery? Personally, I hope so, but this is a question of counterfactual history and as students of history we must deal with what actually transpired. Even by the standards of his own day Whitefield was quite wrong in his support of slavery.

The Bluntisham Awakening
One final example of the impact of Whitefield's preaching relates to a time after his death. Coxe Feary (1759–1822) grew up in the village of Bluntisham, then in Huntingdonshire, about fifteen miles north of Cambridge.[64] He was raised in the Church of England but during his teens became dissatisfied with the irreligious conduct of those who attended worship in the local parish church. He initially thought of attending a Particular Baptist work at a nearby village—it may well have been that at Needingworth a Baptist cause had been founded in 1767. But, in his own words, he found some in the church were "narrow-minded and illiberal" high Calvinists who pronounced "destruction on all who did not believe their creed."[65] For a while he attended a Quaker congregation in Earith, another nearby village, because their views were in accord with his belief in the freedom of the human will and the saving merit of good works. In 1780, though, he read James Hervey's *Theron and Aspasio* (1755), a massive defense of Calvinism. The book was a major challenge to Feary's religious notions and he found himself deeply disturbed by the book's arguments. Offended by the work, he put it down without finishing it. Two years later, though,

---

63. James Walvin, *England, Slaves and Freedom, 1776–1838* (Jackson, MS: University Press of Mississippi, 1986), 103–4. See also, though, the qualifications of David Hempton, "Evangelicalism and Reform, c. 1780–1832" in John Wolffe, ed., *Evangelical Faith and Public Zeal: Evangelicals and Society in Britain 1780–1980* (London: SPCK, 1995), 17–37.

64. For the following story of the Bluntisham Awakening, I am indebted to R. W. Dixon, *A Century of Nonconformity at Bluntisham, Hunts. 1787 to 1887* (Cambridge: Cambridge University Press, 1887), 143–254.

65. Dixon, *Century of Nonconformity*, 169.

he felt impressed to pick up the book again and give it a fair hearing. The result was glorious, nothing less than his conversion.

Along with his conversion he discovered a passion for the salvation of the lost in his village. To one of his neighbors, for instance, he wrote the following plain words in 1783:

> I must beg you to attend to the Scriptures, and to pray to God that he may enlighten your mind by his Holy Spirit, that you may see the gracious privileges contained therein. They, my friend, are the only rule for us to walk by—they testify of Christ—point him out as the only procuring cause of a sinner's acceptance with God, and his enjoyment of eternal felicity. He hath made peace through the blood of his cross, and through that blood we have redemption. It is with regret of mind, my friend, that I think of your carelessness, for I have a great desire for your everlasting welfare, which has been my chief motive for writing to you. Therefore, examine yourself impartially—consider how your affairs stand with God, and see if you have an interest in the merits of Christ; for if you have not, (I dare not flatter you,) you are in a state of death. I hope, therefore, you will say, "What must I do to be saved?" I shall reply, "Believe on the Lord Jesus Christ, and you shall be saved."[66]

By 1784 he was sitting under the evangelical preaching of Henry Venn (1724-1797), the Anglican minister at Yelling, about ten miles away. That same year he came across the works of George Whitefield in a bookshop in St. Ives, where he had gone on a market day. What is amazing is that he had never heard of Whitefield or of his remarkable ministry. So taken was he with the sermons of the great evangelist that the very evening he had purchased them he read one of them aloud to a small gathering of shepherds and farm laborers in his house.

An impact must have been made on some there that night by his reading of this sermon—Whitefield's "What think ye of Christ?"—for the following evening a man of means in the village, a certain John Kent, turned up with several others to hear Feary read another sermon. Flustered in the presence of so many, and afraid he might be considered "a Methodist preacher," Feary refused to read. But the impromptu congregation would not take no for an answer, so Feary consented. A poor woman was so deeply impacted by Whitefield's

---

66. Cited in Dixon, *Century of Nonconformity*, 172-73.

words that she urged Feary to read yet a third time at her house the following evening. Feary agreed but only on condition that she would tell no one about it. But the thing could not be hid. When he went to the house the following evening it was filled with his neighbors.[67]

In fact, Feary continued reading sermons in that woman's home all through the winter of 1784–1785. In the spring of 1785 they had to move to a larger home to accommodate all of the people who were coming. A genuine spiritual awakening had gripped the village, as numbers in the village were moved to ask that old but utterly vital question, "What must I do to be saved?" It was in this work of revival that the foundation of the Particular Baptist work in Bluntisham was laid. Eventually Feary ran out of sermons to read, having gone through all of Whitefield's as well as those of Hervey to which he had access. So it was that he ventured to expound a section of Scripture himself. A barn had been fitted up for the congregation by John Kent and on December 28, 1786, Coxe Feary and twenty-five other believers joined together to form a church. They came from several of the surrounding villages, including Colne, Somersham, and Woodhurst. Feary was chosen as their first pastor. In time, this congregation identified with the Particular Baptists and consisted of some seven or eight hundred persons when Feary died in 1822. Like Abel, Whitefield continued to speak long after he had gone to glory.

---

67. Dixon, *Century of Nonconformity*, 145–46.

CHAPTER 4

"He Carries Fire Wherever He Goes"
William Grimshaw and the Haworth Revival

The Yorkshireman William Crabtree (1720–1811) never forgot the first time that he heard the preaching of the Anglican William Grimshaw (1708–1763). It was 1743 when Crabtree was twenty-three and the Anglican Evangelical was speaking on the parable of the prodigal son. In the course of the sermon Grimshaw made the observation that "one sin would damn a soul as well as a thousand."[1] Now, Crabtree had done his apprenticeship as a weaver in what he later described as "a wicked village, next door to hell itself, given to Sabbath breaking, drunkenness, profane cursing and swearing." He had not been immune from the sins of his fellow villagers. Upon hearing this one sentence, driven home to his heart by the Spirit of God, he said that he thought his situation was "deplorable." But such was the drawing power of the Spirit of God that he continued to go to Haworth to listen to Grimshaw. In time he was soundly converted and eventually became the first pastor of Westgate Baptist Chapel in Bradford, as well as planting three other West Yorkshire Baptist causes at Halifax, Farsley, and Leeds.[2]

Crabtree was one of thousands who blessed God for the day that they first heard Grimshaw and whose powerful preaching was the means of their conversion. In this chapter we explore some aspects of Grimshaw's life and ministry, as well as indicating how God used this Anglican cleric to help revive the Baptist interest in Yorkshire.

---

1. Faith Cook, *William Grimshaw of Haworth* (Edinburgh: Banner of Truth, 1997), 232.
2. Frank Baker, *William Grimshaw 1708–1763* (London: The Epworth Press, 1963), 270.

Early Days in Lancashire and Cambridge

William Grimshaw was born on September 3, 1708, at Brindle, Lancashire, not far from Preston. There is very little reliable data about his early years, though there is some evidence that his parents, nominal Christians at the time, raised him with a sense of moral responsibility to a holy God.[3] At age seventeen Grimshaw went up to Cambridge, where he was admitted to Christ's College—the college of John Milton (1608–1674)—as a sizar (poor student) in April of 1726. The population of Cambridge at the time was some six thousand, a fraction of today's population. It is important to realize that academic standards at Cambridge during the eighteenth century were not that high. Most of the professors did not lecture or tutor the students but spent their time writing and left the direction of the students' academic studies to tutors or tutorial assistants. Academic requirements for completing a degree course were minimal. Moreover, as John Wesley noted about the moral state of Cambridge University and its counterpart in Oxford: "The moment a young man sets foot in either Oxford or Cambridge he is surrounded by company of all kinds…with loungers and triflers of every sort; with men who no more concern themselves with learning than religion."[4]

During his first couple of years at Cambridge, Grimshaw, however, applied himself to his studies and later described himself at this time as "sober and diligent."[5] But this soon changed as Grimshaw gave way to the moral turpitude of university life. In his own words, he fell in "with bad company" and "learned to drink, swear, and what not."[6] Given his style of living, it is amazing that throughout the latter period he hoped to become a clergyman upon graduation. As he put it, he aimed at such because it would give him a steady source of income, a roof over his head, and bread upon his plate.[7] What theology he had was of the deistic variety, in which the robust Christianity

---

3. Baker, *William Grimshaw*, 16–17.
4. Cited in J. H. Whiteley, *Wesley's England* (London: Epworth Press, 1945), 269.
5. Baker, *William Grimshaw*, 23.
6. Cited in Baker, *William Grimshaw*, 24.
7. Cited in Baker, *William Grimshaw*, 24.

of the Reformers and Puritans was subjected to the scrutiny of human reason and all that seemingly could not pass the test of rationality was rejected or played down. Thus, Grimshaw discarded the very concept of revelation along with Trinitarianism and the deity of Christ.[8]

Despite his evident lack of qualifications to be a minister in the Church of England, Grimshaw was ordained in April of 1731 and proceeded to his first charge, what was then the hamlet of Littleborough, three miles north of Rochdale, Lancashire. He was in this parish but a few months. In September of the same year he moved six miles further north to Todmorden, where he was ordained a priest in the Anglican Church in 1732. The men and women in his parish were described by one contemporary as "wild, uncouth, rugged as their native hills."[9] But it was here at Todmorden that Grimshaw began to be awakened to the fact that he was in a desperate spiritual state.

Awakened to "the Pardoning Love of God"
The godlessness of Grimshaw's life was typical of far too many eighteenth-century clerics in the Church of England. Like many other ministers throughout the length and breadth of England, Grimshaw spent his time fishing and hunting, drinking and playing cards. Instead of being times of spiritual nurture, his pastoral visits were occasions for heavy drinking.[10] And like other ministers of this ilk, he thought nothing of the vows he had made when ordained to preach the gospel and to be the spiritual guide of those in the parish. John Newton (1725–1807), who wrote an early biography of Grimshaw, noted that he did "his duty, as the phrase is, in the church, once on the Lord's day…. With this his conscience was satisfied. Whether his flock was satisfied, he neither knew nor cared."[11]

How then was he awakened and converted? In part, the cause of his awakening was the death of a five-week-old girl, the first child of

---

8. Cook, *William Grimshaw*, 12–13.
9. Cited in Baker, *William Grimshaw*, 28.
10. Paul and Faith Cook, *Living the Christian Life: Selected Thoughts of William Grimshaw of Haworth* (Darlington, England; Webster, NY: Evangelical Press, 2008), 13.
11. John Newton, *Memoirs of the Life of the Late Rev. William Grimshaw, A.B.* (London: T. Hamilton, 1814), 8.

a young couple in the parish, James and Susan Scholfield. The mother awoke one awful morning to find the child she dearly loved stone dead. For a period of time Susan's mind became unhinged and she continued to tend to the child as if it were alive. Grimshaw was called for but could only advise the parents "to put away all gloomy thoughts, and to get into merry company, and divert themselves, and all would soon be right."[12] Not surprisingly, this advice proved utterly ineffective to help the parents overcome their grief. Grimshaw was again sent for and this time admitted he did not know what to say to help them.

This realization of his profound lack of spirituality was the first step on the road to change. Grimshaw now tried to reform his life and began to urge his congregation to lead moral lives. He started praying four times a day, a practice he would continue after his conversion. But as he later admitted, all of this was but an earnest "working out a righteousness of his own," in which he tried to balance the sins of his life with good deeds. He actually kept a folio volume, in which he would record his sins on one page and his good deeds on another, with the hope that at year's end they would balance.[13] Although accurate dating is not possible, it seems he went on like this for seven years, from 1734 to 1741. Sometimes, though, the futility of trying to find salvation through the pathway of good works would overwhelm him and he would despair. Once he actually cried out in the middle of a service: "My friends, we are in a damnable state, and I scarcely know how we are to get out of it."[14] He was beginning to realize, in the words of Frank Baker, that "he could not put himself right with God by a multitude of devotional exercises, however arduous."[15]

During this period of time, in 1735, Grimshaw was married to a widow named Sarah Sutcliffe (1710–1739), whom he loved dearly, but who, after bearing him two children, died at the very young age of twenty-nine.[16] Grimshaw was shattered. He went through months of

---

12. Baker, *William Grimshaw*, 29–30.
13. Baker, *William Grimshaw*, 37.
14. Cited in Cook, *William Grimshaw*, 20.
15. Baker, *William Grimshaw*, 39.
16. Baker, *William Grimshaw*, 34–39; Cook, *William Grimshaw*, 20–22.

deep depression—not only mourning for his wife but also sorrowing over his sinful state. He was harassed with sexual temptations, which he resisted, but which left him deeply troubled. Old deistic notions reappeared. On one occasion, for example, he "was tempted to believe Christ to be but a mere man." On another, the thought entered his mind that the God of the Bible was "a cruel implacable Being."[17]

In the midst of this despair God sent him deliverance through "the agency of a man and a book."[18] Although Grimshaw does not specifically identify the man, it may well have been the Yorkshire evangelist Benjamin Ingham (1712–1772), a friend of John Wesley and the brother-in-law of that wealthy patroness of evangelical causes, Selina Hastings (1707–1791).[19] Ingham had been ordained in 1735 and had accompanied John and Charles Wesley as a missionary to the American colony of Georgia. In 1737, after his return to his native town of Ossett in Yorkshire and upon an evangelical conversion, Ingham started to establish what has become known as the Inghamite Methodists after being banned in 1739 from preaching in Anglican churches. By 1755 there were over eighty Inghamite congregations, mainly in Yorkshire and Lancashire. Whether it was Ingham or not, this minister used to ride over to see Grimshaw and rebuke him for his attempts to earn salvation: "Mr. Grimshaw, you are a Jew, you are no believer in Jesus Christ, you are building on the sand."[20]

The book was *The Doctrine of Justification by Faith Through the Imputation of the Righteousness of Christ, Explained, Confirmed, & Vindicated* by the Puritan divine John Owen.[21] Visiting a friend in 1741, Grimshaw happened to see the book lying on a table. Seeing from the title on the spine that it was a theological work, he picked it up and went to open it to the title page. Then a strange event

---

17. Baker, *William Grimshaw*, 41.
18. Baker, *William Grimshaw*, 44.
19. For this identification, see Baker, *William Grimshaw*, 44.
20. Cited in Baker, *William Grimshaw*, 44. On Ingham, see especially H. M. Pickles, *Benjamin Ingham: Preacher Amongst the Dales of Yorkshire, the Forests of Lancashire, and the Fells of Cumbria* (Coventry: H. M. Pickles, 1995).
21. John Owen, *The Doctrine of Justification by Faith Through the Imputation of the Righteousness of Christ, Explained, Confirmed, & Vindicated* (London: R. Boulter, 1677).

happened. As he was opening the book he felt "an uncommon heat" flush his face. Thinking that the flash of heat must have come from a fire in the fireplace of the room, he turned toward it but realized that it was too far away to have caused the flash of heat. He opened the book again and experienced a second heat flash. He took these flashes of heat to be divine signs that this book would be of special help to him.[22] And so it proved.

In this classic study of the imputed righteousness of Christ, Owen argued that justification meant that the sinner who was justified no longer sought to commend himself to God through his own good deeds, but rested in the fact that the righteousness of Christ was reckoned to him, giving him a spotless holiness purer than an angel's. Reading Owen, Grimshaw was enabled, as he later put it, to "renounce myself, every degree of fancied merit and ability, and to embrace Christ only for my all in all. O what light and comfort did I now enjoy in my own soul, and what a taste of the pardoning love of God!"[23]

A couple of decades later, when the London evangelical William Romaine (1714–1795) asked Grimshaw for a statement of his doctrinal convictions, Grimshaw stated the following with regard to Christ's imputed righteousness:

> [T]his very righteousness is sufficient to redeem all mankind; but it only is, and will be imputed to every penitent, believing soul.... Glory be to God for free grace. No reason can be assigned for this; only He would have mercy; because He would have mercy…in this righteousness, every member of Christ stands, and will stand, complete, irreprovable,[24] and acceptable in God's sight, both at death and judgement.[25]

---

22. Cook, *William Grimshaw*, 26–27.
23. Cited in Baker, *William Grimshaw*, 46. For a summary of Owen's work, see A. Skevington Wood, *William Grimshaw* (The Annual Lecture of the Evangelical Library; London: The Evangelical Library, 1963), 12–13.
24. That is, blameless.
25. William Grimshaw's Creed, art. XVI–XVII in his Letter to William Romaine, December 8, 1762, in Erasmus Middleton, *Biographia Evangelica* (London: W. Justins, 1786), 4:411. The spelling and punctuation have been modernized. For the full creed see also Cook, *William Grimshaw*, 315–22.

The Haworth Revival

Grimshaw's preaching now began to change as he heralded forth the good news of salvation by faith alone. Within a year of his conversion in 1741, Grimshaw had moved to a new parish, that of Haworth in West Yorkshire. Haworth was an isolated town in what was then a very hilly and bleak part of Yorkshire. Daily existence there was rough and hard, with life expectancy being around twenty-five. Almost half of all the children in the town died before the age of six. Raw sewage flowed down the main street and contaminated the drinking water, and not surprisingly dysentery and typhus were rampant in the town, along with that killer of the eighteenth century, smallpox.[26] People sought refuge in drink, gambling, and violence. According to John Newton, the inhabitants of the town "had little more sense of religion than their cattle, and were wild and uneducated like the mountains and rocks which surrounded them."[27] Hard and independent, few of Grimshaw's parishioners exhibited any Christian virtues.[28] But Grimshaw was just the man to reach them.

Heralding the changes about to take place in the village was the installation of a new pulpit in the parish church, St. Michael and All Angels. On the sounding board above the pulpit can still be read the two verses of Scripture that Grimshaw had engraved on it to graphically display the heart of his ministry: "I am determined not to know any thing among you, save Jesus Christ, and him crucified" (1 Cor. 2:2) and "For to me to live is Christ, and to die is gain" (Phil. 1:21).[29]

Grimshaw was an extremely gifted preacher who could hold the attention of a congregation for up to two hours while he preached.[30] In part this was because he would use what his critics called "market language" to appeal to his hearers' consciences. He was not afraid of using colloquial words in the pulpit or of even coining new ones. Filled with pithy phrases and striking images, his style of preaching

---

26. Faith Cook, "William Grimshaw—Man of Faith and Action" (unpublished paper, The Carey Conference, Swanwick, Derbyshire, January 9, 2008), 2.
27. Newton, *Memoirs*, 13–14, 43–44.
28. Cook, *Living the Christian Life*, 18–19.
29. Cook, *William Grimshaw*, 58.
30. Cook, *William Grimshaw*, 91; Baker, *William Grimshaw*, 128.

was well suited to drive home the gospel to the hearts of rough and ready Yorkshire men and women. But the success of his preaching was also due to the sense of the presence of God as he would denounce sin, warn of the dreadful consequences of continuing in it, and urge all and sundry to accept Christ as their only hope of salvation.

Only a handful of Grimshaw's sermons survive. A section of his treatise *The Admonition of a Sinner* gives one a taste of his preaching style:

> My neighbour, my friend, my heart longs over you. Your manner of life is actually, openly and evidently such that if not seasonably prevented, it will shortly and certainly terminate in your inevitable, intolerable, eternal ruin and destruction…. Don't be angry with me, please don't. It's because I love you that I thus address you…I want you without delay to repent of your sins, "to seek the Lord while he may be found, to call upon him while he is near" (Isaiah 55:6–7). Acquaint yourself with him, be at peace with him, through his blood, that thereby good may come to you: pardon, peace, grace, heaven, glory, glory for evermore.[31]

At first Grimshaw was unaware that the Haworth Revival was a rivulet in a much larger stream of revival inundating the British Isles in the mid-eighteenth century. But soon he made contact with George Whitefield and the Wesley brothers and became a central figure in the Awakening. Frank Baker has maintained that apart from the evangelists just mentioned, Grimshaw exercised "probably a more potent influence than that of almost any other religious leader of his time."[32] John Wesley was so taken with Grimshaw's love for Christ and his passion for the salvation of sinners that he once wrote, "A few such as him would make a nation tremble. He carries fire wherever he goes."[33] In fact, Wesley nominated Grimshaw as his

---

31. William Grimshaw, *The Admonition of a Sinner* (unpublished manuscript, John Rylands University Library of Manchester). Cited in Esther Bennett, *Heavenly Fire: The Life and ministry of William Grimshaw of Haworth (1708–1763)* (Dundas, ON: Joshua Press, 2000), 8.

32. Baker, *William Grimshaw*, 268.

33. Cited in Cook, *William Grimshaw*, 1.

successor in leading the Arminian Methodist movement if he and Charles were to predecease Grimshaw.³⁴

Within a few months of Grimshaw's arrival in Haworth, the church began to fill with people and conversions become increasingly common. When he had first come to the church in 1742, he had had a dozen or so people taking Communion in a church that could seat twelve hundred. Five years later, the church was full, and twelve hundred took Communion.³⁵ By the late 1740s and early 1750s, summer congregations might reach as high as six thousand! When Whitefield preached at the church in September 1749, for example, over a thousand took Communion and six thousand gathered to hear him preach.³⁶

The people came from all around the countryside. Some were reached by Grimshaw himself as he traveled through the week to various nearby towns and villages outside of the boundaries of his own parish. Others came through the preaching of various lay preachers whom he began to employ from 1744 onwards.³⁷ In any given month of 1751, for instance, Grimshaw reckoned that he might preach some sixty times.³⁸ From the point of view of Anglicanism, this was highly irregular and a source of worry to neighboring parish ministers. To prevent Grimshaw acting irregularly, some of them had recourse to aiding and abetting violent persecution. George White (d. 1751), the nearby vicar of Colne, actually raised a squad of local thugs who were pledged "for the defence of the Church of England" and determined to wreak violence upon either Grimshaw or one of his lay preachers if they preached in the adjoining parishes.³⁹

Consider the experience, for example, of Grimshaw's lay preacher Thomas Lee (1727–1786):

---

34. Cook, *William Grimshaw*, 1, 172, 247.
35. Cook, *William Grimshaw*, 66.
36. Baker, *William Grimshaw*, 182.
37. Cook, *William Grimshaw*, 85.
38. Cook, "William Grimshaw—Man of Faith and Action," 4.
39. Cook, *William Grimshaw*, 127. On the persecution, see Baker, *William Grimshaw*, 130–38.

In the year 1752, and during the winter following, the work of God prospered exceedingly; but persecution raged on every side....One day, as I was going through Pateley [Bridge], the captain of the mob [there], who was kept in constant pay, pursued me, and pulled me off my horse. The mob then soon collected about me; and... dragged me into a house by the hair of the head; then pushed me back, with one or two upon me, and threw me with the small of my back upon the edge of the stone stairs. This nearly broke my back; and it was not well for many years after. Thence they dragged me to the common sewer, which carries the dirt of the town to the river. They rolled me in it for some time; then dragged me to the bridge and threw me into the water. They had me mostly on the ground, my strength being quite spent.

My wife, with some friends, now came up. Seeing her busy about me, some asked: "What, are you a Methodist?"—gave her several blows which made her bleed at the mouth, and swore they would put her into the river. All this time I lay upon the ground, the mob being undetermined what to do. Some cried out: "Make an end of him"—others were for sparing my life; but the dispute was cut short by their agreeing to put some others into the water. So they took them away, leaving me and my wife together. She endeavoured to raise me up; but, having no strength, I dropped to the ground again, and supported me about a hundred yards; then I was set on horseback, and made a shift to ride softly as far as Michael Granger's house. Here I was stripped from head to foot, and was washed. I left my wet clothes here, and rode to Greenhow Hill, where many were waiting for me; and though much bruised and very weak, preached a short sermon from Psalm xxxiv.19: "Many are the troubles of the righteous; but the Lord delivereth him out of them all."[40]

"Mad Grimshaw"

In addition to solid biblical proclamation, Grimshaw's methods for raising the spiritual temperature of the Haworth parish also included what Frank Baker has termed "holy pranks," by reason of which some called the Haworth minister "Mad Grimshaw."[41] For example, John Newton recorded that during Sunday worship Grimshaw sometimes had the congregation sing a psalm—later embellishment made it

---

40. Cited in Bennett, *Heavenly Fire*, 13.
41. Baker, *William Grimshaw*, 13.

Psalm 119—while he went out and checked the inns in the town to see if there were any drinking there who should have been in church.[42] Once he apparently sent two of his churchwardens to round up such loiterers. They were slow in returning so Grimshaw went in search of them. The psalm was long over when footsteps were heard and the two churchwardens appeared shamefaced with Grimshaw behind them. As Grimshaw came into the church he cried out, "What think you! The churchwardens who went out to detect others and prevent them from sinning I have found in the inn drinking a pint of ale! For shame! For shame! For shame!"[43]

On another occasion Grimshaw was striding over the moors to preach in a village some distance from Haworth. Two ruffians met him on the way and sizing him up as one like themselves—for he was a big man physically, broad chested and exceptionally strong[44]—they informed him that they were off "to hear Mad Grimshaw. We shall have some rare sport tonight!" Grimshaw pretended to be heading for another destination, but eventually agreed to accompany them. They had no idea who he truly was until he got to the place where he was to preach and went into the pulpit. The two would-be hecklers were silenced, "first by fear, then by shame, and lastly by the conviction of their own sinfulness, as he rallied them with the words: 'Come on! We shall have some rare sport tonight!'"[45]

John Newton also tells the account of how Grimshaw put an end to the horse racing that was an annual feature of a fair normally held in mid-October. It was, in Grimshaw's words, "a scene of the grossest and most vulgar riot, profligacy, and confusion." Grimshaw sought in vain to end the races, but he did not succeed until in 1759 he made it a matter of extended prayer. That year, quite contrary to the usual pattern of weather for October, it rained incessantly for five days, from

---

42. Newton, *Memoirs*, 93–94. For the embellishment see Cook, *William Grimshaw*, 140–41.

43. Baker, *William Grimshaw*, 212.

44. Baker, *William Grimshaw*, 259.

45. Baker, *William Grimshaw*, 13.

October 12 to October 17. Newton said that it was reported that "old Grimshaw put a stop to the races by his prayers."[46]

"Dissent Warmed Its Hands at Grimshaw's Fire"[47]

Grimshaw's impact on the Particular Baptist cause in Yorkshire was profound. Like far too many other centers of Particular Baptist witness in England during the eighteenth century, many of the Yorkshire Baptists were moribund prior to Grimshaw's ministry.[48] A goodly number of Grimshaw's converts became Baptists, including such Baptist leaders as William Crabtree, mentioned above, Richard Smith (1710–1764) of Wainsgate, James Hartley (1722–1780) of Haworth, and John Parker (1725–1793) of Barnoldswick.[49] Grimshaw, though, took it all in his stride and was even able to joke about the fact that "so many of my chickens turn ducks!"[50]

Grimshaw's greatest influence on Baptist life and witness in Yorkshire, however, came through one who was not converted under his preaching, but who regularly went to hear him for a time, namely John Fawcett (1740–1817). Fawcett was born on January 6, 1740, at Lidget Green, a small village near Bradford in the West Riding of Yorkshire.[51] The death of his father, Stephen Fawcett, when he was but twelve and to whom he was deeply attached, made a deep impression upon him. For some time afterwards he was, his son relates, "deeply

---

46. Newton, *Memoirs*, 103–104. See also Baker, *William Grimshaw*, 213–14.
47. Baker, *William Grimshaw*, 270.
48. See below, chap. 7.
49. For details on Smith and Hartley see Robin Greenwood, "The Evangelical Revival Among Particular Baptists: The Early History of West Lane and Hall Green Baptist Chapels in Haworth, during the Involvement of the Greenwood Family (unpublished manuscript, 2000), 18–29. For Smith, also see Pickles, *Benjamin Ingham*, 40–42. For Parker, see John Fawcett, "A Sketch of the Life and Character of The late Mr. John Parker" in John Parker, *Letters to his Friends* (Leeds, 1794), 3–48.
50. Baker, *William Grimshaw*, 243.
51. The main source for the life of Fawcett is that drawn up by his son [John Fawcett, Jr.] *An Account of the Life, Ministry, and Writings of the Late Rev. John Fawcett, D.D.* (London: Baldwin, Cradock, and Joy; Halifax: P. K. Holden, 1818). See also "Memoir of the Author" in *The Miscellaneous Works of the Late John Fawcett, D.D.* (London: W. Jones, 1824), 3–34 and Ian Sellers, "Other Times, Other Ministries: John Fawcett and Alexander McLaren," *The Baptist Quarterly* 32 (1986–1987): 181–87.

agitated by fears" concerning his father's final state and he prayed much about it.[52] Reinforcing this early openness to spiritual matters was Fawcett's ardent reading of the Scriptures and a variety of Puritan classics, including *Pilgrim's Progress* by John Bunyan (1628–1688), *A Call to the Unconverted to Turn and Live* by Richard Baxter, and the works of John Flavel (ca. 1630–1691). It was not until September 1755, however, that Fawcett understood and owned as his own the biblical way of salvation by "a God reconciled through the atonement of a suffering Saviour."[53] The key influence at this point was not another author from the Puritan era, but one who has been rightly described as a "revived Puritan," namely George Whitefield.[54] Converted under the preaching of Whitefield, Fawcett kept a portrait of the evangelist in his study and "the very mention of his name inspired the warmest emotions of grateful remembrance."[55] Fawcett was personally convinced of many of the emphases of the Evangelical Revival and would in time become a powerful force for the revival of the Particular Baptists in the north of England.

For the two years following, Fawcett frequently used to trudge the nine or so miles over the moors from Bradford to hear Grimshaw and especially made a point of going when the Lord's Supper was to be administered.[56] In 1764 Fawcett was called to succeed Richard Smith as pastor of Wainsgate Baptist Church in Hebden Bridge, where many of the early members, including Smith, had come to Christ under Grimshaw's powerful ministry. Located but five or six miles from Haworth, this church can be considered a direct result of the Haworth Revival.

Fawcett's ministry here and then later in a work right in the town of Hebden Bridge was marked by an irenic Calvinism and catholicity—both marks of the life of Grimshaw as well—a robust commitment to theological education—he began an academy for training Baptist ministers—and missions—William Ward (1769–1823), who went out

---

52. [Fawcett, Jr.], *Life, Ministry, and Writings*, 6–7.
53. [Fawcett, Jr.], *Life, Ministry, and Writings*, 16.
54. [Fawcett, Jr.], *Life, Ministry, and Writings*, 15–17.
55. [Fawcett, Jr.], *Life, Ministry, and Writings*, 15.
56. [Fawcett, Jr.], *Life, Ministry, and Writings*, 30–31.

to India to join William Carey (1761–1834) at Serampore, was trained under Fawcett.[57] In fact, without a gift of £200 that Fawcett gave to the fledgling Baptist Missionary Society in 1793, it is quite possible that Carey would not have been able to sail to India that year.[58] In a way, then, Grimshaw played a small role in the onset of the modern missionary movement. The Yorkshire cleric would have rejoiced in the thought of Carey preaching Christ in India, for, as he wrote in the creed he sent to William Romaine, Christ's imputed "righteousness is sufficient to redeem all mankind."[59]

---

57. Baker, *William Grimshaw*, 271.
58. George R. Cragg, *Grimshaw of Haworth: A Study in Eighteenth Century Evangelicalism* (London; Edinburgh: Canterbury Press, 1947), 102.
59. Cragg, *Grimshaw of Haworth*, 103.

CHAPTER 5

"The Theologian of Revival"
Becoming Jonathan Edwards

The writings of the New England divine Jonathan Edwards (1703–1758) are of especial importance when it comes to the subject of the Holy Spirit's work in revival because he is, as Martyn Lloyd-Jones once described him, "preeminently the theologian of Revival."[1] His writings on revival possess ongoing value because, first of all, they are rooted in a personal and intimate acquaintance with revival. The earliest letter that we possess from his hand, written to his elder sister Mary when he was but twelve years of age, tells of a revival in his hometown of East Windsor, Connecticut, under the preaching of his father, Timothy Edwards (1669–1758). He describes it as "a very remarkable stirring and pouring out of the Spirit of God" in which it was common on Mondays, after the Word had been preached the day before, for "above thirty persons to speak with Father about the condition of their souls."[2] More significantly, the revival that made a profound impact on the Connecticut Valley during the winter of 1734–1735, which we shall look at later in this chapter, began in Edwards's church in Northampton, Massachusetts, and was subsequently described and analyzed in his *A Faithful Narrative of the Surprising Work of God in the Conversion*

---

1. D. Martyn Lloyd-Jones, "Jonathan Edwards and the Crucial Importance of Revival" in his *The Puritans: Their Origins and Successors*, 361. In the words of J. I. Packer, Edwards's theology of revival "is, perhaps, the most important single contribution that Edwards has to make to evangelical thinking today," *Quest for Godliness*, 316. See also the remarks in this regard by Davies, *I Will Pour Out My Spirit*, 26: "No one who studies the topic of revival will dispute the statement that Jonathan Edwards, the eighteenth-century American preacher and writer, is the classic theologian on the subject."

2. "The Earliest Known Letter of Jonathan Edwards," *Christian History* 4, no. 4 (1985): 34.

of Many Hundred Souls in Northampton, and the Neighbouring Towns and Villages of New [sic] *Hampshire in New-England* (1737). Over a hundred years later this powerful book was still being consulted as a handbook on the nature of revival.[3]

Five years after this regional revival there occurred what is known as the Great Awakening, the revival that swept the entirety of the American colonies from 1740 to 1742. Although the English itinerant evangelist George Whitefield was the main human instrument in this revival, Edwards also played a very prominent role in it. He too traveled and preached extensively beyond the borders of his Northampton church.[4] Even more significantly, in print Edwards was this revival's most theologically astute champion as well as its most perceptive critic. This dual role in the revival called forth some of Edwards's finest books. Among these works are ones that are still regarded as Christian classics, of which the most notable is *A Treatise Concerning Religious Affections* (1746).

Edwards's reflections on the work of the Spirit are still of immense value because Edwards possessed a wonderful facility for meticulous and minute observation. This facility can be seen in the intriguing and detailed investigation which he conducted during the early 1720s into the way that spiders made their webs.[5] Later in his life, this gift, now exercised in the realm of pastoral ministry and theology, yielded a profound understanding of the human heart and its workings. Sereno E. Dwight (1786–1850), Edwards's great-grandson and one of his early biographers, stated that Edwards's "knowledge of the human heart, and its operations, has scarcely been equalled by that of any uninspired preacher." Dwight went on to mention three probable sources for this insightful understanding of the human heart: Edwards's perceptive reading of the Scriptures; "his thorough

---

3. John E. Smith, *Jonathan Edwards: Puritan, Preacher, Philosopher* (Notre Dame, IN: University of Notre Dame Press, 1992), 5.

4. Helen Westra, *The Minister's Task and Calling in the Sermons of Jonathan Edwards* (Lewiston, NY; Queenston, ON: The Edwin Mellen Press, 1986), 34.

5. Jonathan Edwards, *The Spider Letter* in John E. Smith, Harry S. Stout, and Kenneth P. Minkema, eds., *A Jonathan Edwards Reader* (New Haven, CT; London: Yale University Press, 1995), 1–8.

acquaintance with his own heart"; and his grasp of philosophy.[6] It should not be surprising that this combination of personal experience and empirical insight—thoroughly rooted in Scripture—produced some of the most significant literature on the Spirit's work in revival in the history of the church. To quote Lloyd-Jones again: "If you want to know anything about the psychology of religion, conversion, revivals, read Jonathan Edwards."[7]

One further reason for the classic nature of Edwards's corpus of work on revival is the fact that Jonathan Edwards was blessed with a heart devoted to the pursuit of the glory of God. "The great end of God's works," Edwards wrote, "is most properly and comprehensively called, the glory of God."[8] According to Joseph G. Haroutunian, even "a superficial perusal of the essays and sermons of Edwards reveals a mind passionately devoted to God, permeated with the beauty and excellence of God."[9] Haroutunian cited as an example in this regard the following passage from the sermon *Ruth's Resolution*, which Edwards preached during the Northampton Revival of 1734–1735 and which was published three years later. Reflecting on Ruth's determination to cleave to her mother-in-law Naomi and to embrace her God, the God of Israel, as her own (Ruth 1:16), Edwards stated that this God is a "glorious God":

> There is none like him, who is infinite in glory and excellency. He is the most high God, glorious in holiness, fearful in praises, doing wonders. His name is excellent in all the earth, and his glory is above the heavens. Among the gods there is none like unto him; there is none in heaven to be compared to him, nor are there any among the sons of the mighty that can be likened unto him.... God

---

6. Dwight, "Memoirs of Jonathan Edwards, A. M.," 1:clxxxix. I owe this reference to John Piper, *The Supremacy of God in Preaching* (Grand Rapids: Baker, 1990), 95–96. Piper has some good comments on this aspect of Edwards's ministry; see Piper, *Supremacy of God*, 95–98.

7. Lloyd-Jones, "Jonathan Edwards and the Crucial Importance of Revival," *The Puritans*, 361.

8. Jonathan Edwards, *A Dissertation Concerning the End for which God Created the World* in *Works of Jonathan Edwards*, 1:119.

9. Joseph G. Haroutunian, "Jonathan Edwards: Theologian of the Great Commandment," *Theology Today* 1 (1944): 361.

is the fountain of all good, and an inexhaustible fountain; he is an all-sufficient God, able to protect and defend…and do all things… He is the king of glory, the Lord strong and mighty, the Lord mighty in battle: a strong rock, and a high tower…. He is a God who hath all things in his hands, and does whatsoever he pleases: he killeth and maketh alive; he bringeth down to the grave and bringeth up; he maketh poor and maketh rich: the pillars of the earth are the Lord's…. God is an infinitely holy God; there is none holy as the Lord. And he is infinitely good and merciful. Many that others worship and serve as gods, are cruel beings, spirits that seek the ruin of souls; but this is a God that delighteth in mercy; his grace is infinite, and endures for ever. He is love itself, an infinite fountain and ocean of it.[10]

As Haroutunian noted, this passage is characteristic of Edwards's view of God, especially the focus on God's unique excellency and the fact that the God whom the believer seeks to glorify and serve is "the Creator of the universe and the Fountain of all beauty and excellence."[11] This God-centered perspective led Edwards to support and promote the revivals of his day, because he saw God at work in them, bringing glory to Himself.[12] Written from this perspective, these works on revival have been recognized by later evangelical authors as providing something of a benchmark for reflection on the nature of spiritual awakening.[13] Contemporary evangelicalism, largely indifferent to the glory and beauty of God, sorely needs to ponder this rich and profound corpus of literature on revival.

Edwards's Early Years

Born on October 5, 1703, at East Windsor, Connecticut, Jonathan Edwards was the fifth of his parents' eleven children—ten girls and Jonathan![14] Edwards's sisters grew to be tall women and those

---

10. Jonathan Edwards, *Ruth's Resolution* in *Works of Jonathan Edwards*, 1:665.
11. Haroutunian, "Jonathan Edwards," 362.
12. Mark A. Noll, *The Scandal of the Evangelical Mind* (Grand Rapids: Eerdmans; Leicester: InterVarsity Press, 1994), 77–80.
13. Davies, *I Will Pour Out My Spirit*, 36–39.
14. Especially helpful for understanding Edwards's life are Iain H. Murray, *Jonathan Edwards: A New Biography* (Edinburgh: Banner of Truth, 1987) and George Marsden, *Jonathan Edwards: A Life* (New Haven, CT; London: Yale University Press, 2003).

who knew them often spoke of Timothy Edwards's "sixty feet of daughters."[15] Their father encouraged them to develop both intellectually and spiritually.[16] In fact, in his early childhood Jonathan was tutored by his older sisters.[17] Iain Murray in his biography of Edwards reckons that the preponderance of females in Edwards's early years helped shape the "gentleness of Jonathan's bearing in later life."[18] Actually, the Edwards sisters were strong, single-minded women, who were not afraid to speak their minds. For instance, during the Great Awakening (1740–1742), in which Jonathan Edwards played a key role, his eldest sister Esther (1695–1766) was firmly opposed to the revival. In a diary entry for August 1743 she noted, "I was last night in company with one of the 'New Lights.' I could hardly bear the room." Nor did she keep her views to herself and enclosed in her diary. The following March, she made known her problems with the revival to her brother, and they had a strong disagreement about the awakening. In her diary, she wrote, "Some things occurred this morning which made it appear very doubtful whether my dear brother would ever come off of some principles which appeared to me were detrimental to religion."[19] On the other hand, his sisters were also women of great piety. Before her early death, Jerusha (1710–1729), one of Jonathan's younger sisters, was known for her "solitary meditations, contemplative walks in the woods, and late-night Scripture readings."[20]

Like his sisters, Edwards received his elementary education and a thorough nurture in Puritan piety from his father. In Edwards's *Personal Narrative* he notes of this time in his life:

> I had a variety of concerns and exercises about my soul from my childhood; but had two more remarkable seasons of awakening.... The first time was when I was a boy, some years before I went to

---

15. Murray, *Jonathan Edwards*, 9.
16. On Jonathan's sisters, see Kenneth P. Minkema, "Hannah and Her Sisters: Sisterhood, Courtship, and Marriage in the Edwards Family in the Early Eighteenth Century," *The New England Historical and Genealogical Register* 146 (January 1992): 35–56.
17. Minkema, "Hannah and Her Sisters," 41.
18. Murray, *Jonathan Edwards*, 9.
19. Minkema, "Hannah and Her Sisters," 42.
20. Minkema, "Hannah and Her Sisters," 38.

college, at a time of a remarkable awakening in my father's congregation.... I used to pray five times a day in secret, and to spend much time in religious talk with other boys; and used to meet with them to pray together.... I, with some of my schoolmates joined together, and built a booth in a swamp, in a very retired spot, for a place of prayer.... My affections seemed to be lively and easily moved, and I seemed to be in my element, when engaged in religious duties.[21]

But this childhood spirituality—albeit a prognostication of his future interests—soon disappeared and, in his words, he "returned like a dog to his vomit, and went on in ways of sin."[22]

In 1716 Edwards entered the Collegiate School of Connecticut in New Haven (later to become Yale University). Although he went on to graduate from the Collegiate School in 1720 at the head of his class academically, Edwards had neither inner peace nor saving faith. Writing later of his life at this time, Edwards said that it was characterized "by great and violent inward struggles" regarding wicked inclinations and objections against God's sovereignty in salvation.[23]

It was probably in the spring of 1721 that Edwards was converted.[24] Edwards later said that, as he was reading 1 Timothy 1:17,[25]

> there came into my soul, and was as it were diffused through it, a sense of the glory of the Divine Being; a new sense, quite different from any thing I ever experienced before. Never any words of scripture seemed to me as these words did. I thought with myself, how excellent a Being that was; and how happy I should be, if I might enjoy that God, and be rapt up to him in Heaven, and be as it were swallowed up in him for ever.... From about that time, I began to have a new kind of apprehensions and ideas of Christ, and the work of redemption, and the glorious way of salvation by him. An inward, sweet sense of these things, at times, came into my heart;

---

21. Jonathan Edwards, *Personal Narrative* in *Jonathan Edwards: Letters and Personal Writings*, ed. George S. Claghorn, *The Works of Jonathan Edwards* (New Haven, CT; London: Yale University Press, 1998), 16:790–91.
22. Edwards, *Personal Narrative*, 16:791.
23. Edwards, *Personal Narrative*, 16:791–92.
24. For the date of Edwards's conversion, see Murray, *Jonathan Edwards*, 35.
25. "Now unto the King eternal, immortal, invisible, the only wise God, be honour and glory for ever and ever. Amen."

and my soul was led away in pleasant views and contemplations of them. And my mind was greatly engaged to spend my time in reading and meditating on Christ, on the beauty and excellency of his person, and the lovely way of salvation, by free grace in him.[26]

One of the noteworthy things about this text is Edwards's mention of the "inward, sweet sense" that gripped his soul as he meditated upon what Scripture says about God and Christ and upon their utterly free and sovereign grace in salvation. Such biblical meditation would become central to his piety. Samuel Hopkins (1721–1803), one of his close friends and his first biographer, noted that Edwards was, "as far as it can be known, much on his knees in secret, and in devout reading of God's word and meditation upon it."[27]

Not long after his conversion Edwards drew up what are known as the *Resolutions* (1722–1723) in which at the outset of his ministry he committed himself to keeping a list of seventy guidelines to help him stay passionate in his pursuit of God and his glory.[28] Though Edwards was young when he wrote them, they bespeak a mature understanding of genuine piety and the way such piety should be evident in all of life and pursued with ardor and zeal. There is one resolution that deals especially with the Scriptures. Resolution 28 stated what he hoped would be a lifelong characteristic of the way he approached Scripture. He declared that he was "[r]esolved, to study the Scriptures so steadily, constantly, and frequently, as that I may find, and plainly perceive, myself to grow in the knowledge of the same."[29] The adverbs Edwards uses here—"steadily, constantly, and frequently"—surely indicate his desire to saturate his mind with Scripture. This pattern of meditation upon God's holy Word, one that was part of Edwards's Puritan heritage, continued to be central to

---

26. Edwards, *Personal Narrative*, 16:792, 793.
27. Samuel Hopkins, "The Life and Character of the Late Reverend Mr. Jonathan Edwards" in *Jonathan Edwards: A Profile*, ed. David Levin (New York: Hill and Wang, 1969), 39.
28. For an accessible edition of the *Resolutions*, see *Jonathan Edwards' Resolutions and Advice to Young Converts*, ed. Stephen J. Nichols (Phillipsburg, NJ: P&R Publishing, 2001).
29. My attention was drawn to this resolution by John Piper, "Saturate...Search," *The Standard* (March 1986): 36.

Edwards's walk with God throughout his life. Samuel Hopkins noted that Edwards "had an uncommon thirst for knowledge, in the pursuit of which, he spared no cost nor pains." He thus "read all the books, especially books of divinity," that he could get hold of. But, Hopkins emphasized, "he studied the Bible more than all other books, and more than most other divines do. His uncommon acquaintance with the Bible appears in his sermons, and in most of his publications; and his great pains in studying it are manifest in his manuscript notes upon it."[30] For Edwards, the Scriptures were thus "the great and standing rule for the direction of his [that is, God's] church in all religious matters, and…in all ages."[31]

The 1734–1735 Northampton Revival

In August 1726 Edwards was invited to become the assistant to his grandfather, Solomon Stoddard (1643–1729), who was the pastor of the Congregationalist church in Northampton, Massachusetts. Two years later, when Stoddard died in 1729, Edwards was called to be the sole pastor of the church. The Northampton church had enjoyed a number of small revivals during Solomon Stoddard's long pastorate, the last one having been in 1718. After that time, though, Edwards judged there had been little in the way of spiritual advance. In his words:

> Just after my grandfather's death, it seemed to be a time of extraordinary dullness in religion. Licentiousness for some years prevailed among the youth of the town; they were many of them very much addicted to night-walking, and frequenting the tavern, and lewd practices, wherein some, by their example, exceedingly corrupted others. It was their manner very frequently to get together, in conventions of both sexes for mirth and jollity, which they called frolics; and they would often spend the greater part of the night in them, without regard to any order in the families they belonged to: and indeed family government did too much fail in the town. It was become very customary with many of our young people to

---

30. Hopkins, "Life and Character of Edwards" in *Jonathan Edwards*, ed. Levin, 40–41.
31. Jonathan Edwards, *The Distinguishing Marks of a Work of the Spirit of God* in *Jonathan Edwards on Revival* (Edinburgh: Banner of Truth, 1984), 113–14.

be indecent in their carriage at meeting, which doubtless would not have prevailed in such a degree, had it not been that my grandfather, through his great age (though he retained his powers, surprisingly to the last), was not so able to observe them. There had also long prevailed in the town a spirit of contention between two parties, into which they had for many years been divided; by which they maintained a jealousy one of the other, and were prepared to oppose one another in all public affairs.[32]

As Edwards notes in this text, the adults in the town were split into two factions, whom one might describe as the "haves" and the "have-nots," those who were wealthy and had property and those who were jealous of them and sought to diminish their power and influence.[33] Most of these adults were taken up not with the things of God and His kingdom but with other cares and pursuits, especially the pursuit of material wealth. Outwardly they were orthodox but they had no inward religion. Their orthodoxy was dry and lifeless. Not surprisingly their children were, in Edwards's own words, "very much addicted to night-walking, and frequenting the tavern, and lewd practices." As American historian Richard Lovelace has noted, if these teens had had drugs, they would have used them.[34] The spiritual lassitude of the inhabitants of Northampton was endemic throughout New England. Moral conditions may not have been as bad as those in Great Britain, yet Oxford historian John Walsh has noted the following characteristics of transatlantic British society in the opening decades of the eighteenth century: a noticeable decay of ministerial authority, the growth of rationalism and a massive intellectual assault on supernatural Christianity, the spread of material wealth and "luxury," the frivolity of the young and an indifference on their part to spiritual matters, and a sense of spiritual powerlessness among both pious Anglicans and Dissenters.[35]

---

32. Jonathan Edwards, *A Faithful Narrative of the Surprising Work of God* in *Jonathan Edwards on Revival*, 9.

33. Murray, *Jonathan Edwards*, 87.

34. Lovelace, *Dynamics of Spiritual Life*, 38.

35. "'Methodism' and the Origins of English-Speaking Evangelicalism" in Mark A. Noll, David W. Bebbingion, and George A. Rawlyk, eds., *Evangelicalism: Comparative Studies of Popular Protestantism in North America, the British Isles, and Beyond, 1700–1990* (New York and Oxford: Oxford University Press, 1994), 20–21.

In the early 1730s, however, there began to be a growing sensitivity to sin and a willingness to listen to religious counsel in Northampton.[36] A series of sermons on justification by faith alone—the doctrine that had been so central to the Reformation—was particularly used of God to awaken the lost and the spiritually indifferent. The series was preached by Edwards in November and December 1734. In these sermons Edwards especially stressed that God, in justifying sinners, does so on the basis of His mercy alone. Those whom God saves are not saved because God sees anything in them that would merit His favor and blessing. To quote Edwards: when God justifies a person He "has no regard to anything in the person justified, as godliness, or any goodness." In fact, Edwards went on to say, "before this act [of justification], God beholds him as an ungodly creature." Justification entails God choosing to reckon Christ's perfect righteousness to the sinner and in this way the sinner can be declared righteous.[37]

Edwards identified the exposition of this central feature of the New Testament as the major catalyst that the Holy Spirit used to begin an extraordinary time of revival in Northampton.

> There were some things said publicly...concerning justification by faith alone.... It proved a word spoken in season here; and was most evidently attended with a very remarkable blessing of heaven to the souls of the people in this town.... And then it was, in the latter part of December [of 1734], that the Spirit of God began extraordinarily to set in, and wonderfully to work amongst us; and there were very suddenly, one after another, five or six persons, who were to all appearances savingly converted, and some of them wrought upon in a very remarkable manner.[38]

Edwards here makes a direct link between the preaching of biblical truth and the onset of revival by his use of the connective "then." It was *after* the preaching of justification by faith alone—which Edwards also denotes as "the way of the gospel...the true and only way"[39]—

---

36. Edwards, *Faithful Narrative*, 9–10.
37. Jonathan Edwards, *Justification by Faith Alone* in *Works of Jonathan Edwards*, 1:622.
38. Edwards, *Faithful Narrative*, 11–12. For a discussion of other subsidiary causes of the revival, see Samuel T. Logan, Jr., "Jonathan Edwards and the 1734–35 Northampton Revival," *Preaching and Revival* (London: The Westminster Conference, 1984), 63–65.
39. Edwards, *Faithful Narrative*, 12.

that the Spirit began to work so "wonderfully" and "suddenly." Soon, Edwards narrated in his account of this revival, an intense concern to be right with God and to walk with Him gripped the town.

> Although people did not ordinarily neglect their worldly business, yet religion was with all sorts the great concern, and the world was a thing only by the bye. The only thing in their view was to get the kingdom of heaven, and every one appeared pressing into it. The engagedness of their hearts in this great concern could not be hid, it appeared in their very countenances. It then was a dreadful thing amongst us to lie out of Christ, in danger every day of dropping into hell; and what persons' minds were intent upon, was to escape for their lives, and to fly from wrath to come. All would eagerly lay hold of opportunities for their souls, and were wont very often to meet together in private houses, for religious purposes: and such meetings when appointed were greatly thronged.[40]

Out of a town of about twelve hundred people, Edwards initially reckoned that some three hundred were saved in about six months.[41] At the revival's height, in March and April of 1735, there were about thirty people a week professing conversion.[42] Edwards would later judge that there were not as many converts as he had thought during the actual time of the revival.[43] Nevertheless, he never doubted that what took place during 1734 and 1735 was a tremendous, God-wrought awakening in the town.

At the time, the impact on the town and church meetings was nothing less than dramatic.

> This work of God, as it was carried on, and the number of true saints multiplied, soon made a glorious alteration in the town: so that…the town seemed to be full of the presence of God: it never was so full of love, nor of joy, and yet so full of distress, as it was then. There were remarkable tokens of God's presence in almost every house. It was a time of joy in families on account of salvation being brought unto them; parents rejoicing over their children

---

40. Edwards, *Faithful Narrative*, 12–13.
41. Edwards, *Faithful Narrative*, 19.
42. Edwards, *Faithful Narrative*, 21.
43. Jonathan Edwards, Letter to Thomas Gillespie, July 1, 1751, in *The Great Awakening*, ed. C. C. Goen, *The Works of Jonathan Edwards* (New Haven, CT; London: Yale University Press, 1972), 4:565.

as new born, and husbands over their wives, and wives over their husbands. The goings of God were then seen in his sanctuary, God's day was a delight, and his tabernacles were amiable. Our public assemblies were then beautiful: the congregation was alive in God's service, every one earnestly intent on the public worship, every hearer eager to drink in the words of the minister as they came from his mouth; the assembly in general were, from time to time, in tears while the word was preached; some weeping with sorrow and distress, others with joy and love, others with pity and concern for the souls of their neighbours.[44]

Nor was the revival limited to the town of Northampton. It spread swiftly to thirty-two other towns throughout the Connecticut River Valley.

Edwards's account of this revival is found in his *A Faithful Narrative of the Surprising Work of God*, which was first published in London in 1737. Among those who read it at that time and were deeply impressed was Howel Harris, who came to possess a copy of the book in February 1738. After reading it he was led to pray, "O go on with Thy work there [that is, in New England] and here."[45] Harris's prayer received an answer in 1740–1742, when God again visited New England with revival, but this time on a much more extensive scale.

The Great Awakening in America, 1740–1742

This revival has come to be known as the Great Awakening. It made a profound impact not only on New England but also on the other American colonies to the south. Estimates of those converted in New England alone, where the population was around 250,000 at the time, range from 25,000 to 50,000. These figures, it should be noted, do not include conversions of those who were already church members.[46] In the middle of the revival William Cooper (1694–1743), one of Edwards's friends and the Congregationalist minister of Brattle

---

44. Edwards, *Faithful Narrative*, 14.
45. Evans, *Daniel Rowland*, 72.
46. Graham D. Harrison, "Ferment in New England: Reactions to the Great Awakening" in *Faith and Ferment* ([London]: The Westminster Conference, 1982), 72.

Street Church, Boston, gave his perspective on what God was doing in his day.

> The dispensation of grace we are now under, is certainly such as neither we nor our fathers have seen; and in some circumstances so wonderful, that I believe there has not been the like since the extraordinary pouring out of the Spirit immediately after our Lord's ascension. The apostolical times seem to have returned upon us: such a display has there been of the power and grace of the divine Spirit in the assemblies of his people, and such testimonies has he given to the word of the gospel.... A number of preachers have appeared among us, to whom God has given such a large measure of his Spirit, that we are ready sometimes to apply to them the character given of Barnabas, that "he was a good man, and full of the Holy Ghost, and of faith" (Acts 11:24). They preach the gospel of the grace of God from place to place, with uncommon zeal and assiduity. The doctrines they insist on are the doctrines of the reformation, under the influence whereof the power of godliness so flourished in the last century. The points on which their preaching mainly turns are those important ones of man's guilt, corruption, and impotence; supernatural regeneration by the Spirit of God, and free justification by faith in the righteousness of Christ; and the marks of the new birth. The manner of their preaching is not with the "enticing words of man's wisdom" (1 Corinthians 2:4); howbeit, they "speak wisdom among them that are perfect" (1 Corinthians 2:6). An ardent love to Christ and souls warms their breasts and animates their labours. God has made those his ministers active spirits, a flame of fire in his service; and his word in their mouths has been, "as a fire, and as a hammer that breaketh the rock in pieces" (Jeremiah 23:29).[47]

Here Cooper placed the revival in New England within the broad sweep of church history. He was utterly convinced that no other revival, in either his lifetime or that of his Puritan forebears, was comparable to what God was doing in the early 1740s. In some respects,

---

47. William Cooper, preface to *Distinguishing Marks*, by Edwards, in *Jonathan Edwards on Revival*, 77–79. See also the comments of Thomas Templeton Taylor, "The Spirit of the Awakening: The Pneumatology of New England's Great Awakening in Historical and Theological Context" (PhD thesis, University of Illinois at Urbana-Champaign, 1988), 233–35. On William Cooper, see William B. Sprague, *Annals of the American Pulpit* (New York, NY: Robert Carter and Brothers, 1857), 1:288–91.

only at the time of Pentecost could one find something genuinely comparable! The preaching through which God had brought about this revival, though, did not contain anything new. Essentially it was the same doctrine of salvation that was trumpeted forth at the time of the Reformation and in the Puritan era, one that highlighted humanity's total depravity, the Spirit's glorious sovereignty in regenerating sinners, and their justification by faith alone in Christ. And the preaching style fit the doctrine: it was plain and ardent.

Cooper went on to specify what he considered so extraordinary about the revival. First, there was the incredible way that it had swept through "some of the most populous towns, the chief places of concourse and business." Then, there were the numbers that had professed conversion: "Stupid sinners have been awakened by hundreds." During the winter of 1740–1741 in Boston alone, Cooper stated, there were "some thousands under such religious impressions as they never felt before." People of all ages, from the very elderly to the very young, had been saved: the elderly "snatched as brands out of the burning, made monuments of divine mercy" and "sprightly youth… made to bow like willows to the Redeemer's sceptre." Moreover, God had drawn to Himself some of the grossest sinners in New England: drunkards, fornicators, and adulterers, people addicted to profanity and "carnal worldlings have been made to seek first the kingdom of God and his righteousness." On the other hand, many of those who deemed themselves upright and moral had become convinced that "morality is not to be relied on for life; and so excited to seek after the new birth, and a vital union to Jesus Christ by faith."[48]

---

48. Cooper, preface to *Distinguishing Marks*, 79–81.

CHAPTER 6

"A Spirit of Powerful Holy Affection"
Twelve Marks of Genuine Revival

During the course of the Great Awakening in America, Jonathan Edwards became conscious that in addition to the work of the Holy Spirit in this remarkable move of God, Satan had also been powerfully active in producing a counterfeit religion. The latter was a religion that made much of experience, "discoveries of Christ," and the work of the Holy Spirit. Knowing that some of his readers would be completely shocked at such assertions, Edwards rightly reasoned that the devil would never trouble himself to counterfeit valueless things: "there are many more counterfeits of silver and gold, than of iron and copper; there are many false diamonds and rubies, but who goes about to counterfeit common stones?"[1] Satan, ever the master of cunning and lies, employs his subtlety in making imitations of the most excellent things. Thus, it is vital to know the marks of genuine Christianity as it is laid out in the Scriptures. Edwards ever longed to make, as he put it, "the Holy Scriptures our rule, in judging of the nature of true religion."[2]

The immediate reason for Edwards's thinking about the nature of true revival were the actions and assertions of James Davenport (1716–1757), who was a minister from Southold, Long Island. In the early stages of the revival his preaching could not be faulted.[3] Itinerating

---

1. Jonathan Edwards, *Religious Affections*, ed. John E. Smith, *The Works of Jonathan Edwards* (New Haven, CT: Yale University Press, 1959), 2:146.

2. Edwards, *Religious Affections*, 314.

3. For a discussion of Davenport's involvement in the revival, see Harry S. Stout and Peter Onuf, "James Davenport and the Great Awakening in New London," *The Journal of American History* 71 (1983–1984): 556–78; Iain H. Murray, *Jonathan Edwards: A New Biography* (Edinburgh: Banner of Truth, 1987), 223–29; Robert E. Cray, Jr., "More Light on

throughout New England he was led, however, into increasingly fanatical attitudes and patterns of behavior. When he came into a town he would interrogate the minister as to his spiritual state. Those who refused to answer his questions or whose answers did not satisfy him he declared to be unconverted and unfit to be spiritual leaders. He then encouraged the members of their congregations to forsake them and conduct their own meetings. Invariably he publicly upbraided those members of the clergy he deemed to be unconverted. For example, at New Haven, Connecticut, he branded the local Congregationalist pastor Joseph Noyes (1688–1761) "an unconverted hypocrite and the devil incarnate."[4] Moreover, those individuals whom he considered regenerate he would call "brother" or "sister," the rest "neighbour." Not surprisingly, wherever Davenport went he left divided congregations in his wake. All of this was rooted in Davenport's claim to have the ability to distinguish who was among the elect of God.

Davenport also began to assure individuals who fell to the ground, or who experienced bodily tremors, or who saw visions while he was preaching that such experiences were a sure sign of the Spirit's converting work. The most bizarre episode of Davenport's career took place in March 1743 in the town of New London, Connecticut, where Davenport and a number of his followers had established a seminary known as the "Shepherd's Tent."[5] Under the guidance "received from the Spirit in dreams," Davenport directed his followers in the afternoon of Sunday, March 6, just as the inhabitants of the town were returning home from public worship, to publicly dissociate themselves from the "heresy" of Puritan New England by burning in a bonfire a large quantity of books. Among the books burnt that day

---

a New Light: James Davenport's Religious Legacy, Eastern Long Island, 1740–1840," *New York History* 73 (1992): 5–27.

4. C. C. Goen, editor's introduction to *The Great Awakening*, in *The Works of Jonathan Edwards* (New Haven, CT; London: Yale University Press, 1972), 4:52.

5. For two firsthand accounts of the New London incident, see Charles Chauncy, *Seasonable Thoughts on the State of Religion in New-England* (1743, Hicksville, NY; The Regina Press, 1975), 220–23, footnote; "Religious Excess at New London: *Boston Weekly Post-Boy*, 1743" in *The Great Awakening: Documents on the Revival of Religion, 1740–1745*, ed. Richard L. Bushman (1970, Chapel Hill, NC; London: University of North Carolina Press for the Institute of Early American History and Culture, 1989), 51–53.

there were said to be works by such well-known Puritans as John Flavel, Matthew Henry, and Increase Mather (1639–1723)! Davenport's followers then proceeded to dance around the bonfire praising God and shouting "Hallelujah" and "Gloria Patri" ("Glory to the Father").

The following day a second bonfire was prepared, this time intended to consume the "idolatry" of Davenport and his followers. Anything that smacked of the "world" and worldly pride—"wigs, cloaks and breeches, hood, gowns, rings, jewels and necklaces"—was heaped up, ready to be consumed. Davenport himself stripped off his "breeches" and hove them onto the pile to be burned. At this point a bystander said to Davenport that he thought him demonized, to which the latter surprisingly agreed. Smitten with contrition for his actions, Davenport soon quit Connecticut for Long Island, a broken and shattered man. On Long Island, Davenport came to his senses, admitted his errors, published a confession of his sins, and actively sought to make restitution. But he had helped to unleash a "wild-fire" spirit that in many places made havoc of the revival.[6] In a sermon that he preached two years before his death in 1757, he was surely thinking of his earlier errors when he stated that among the people of God ministers are subject to greater temptation than others, "as officers in an army are more aim'd at and pointed at by the enemy than private soldiers."[7]

Davenport's antics provided anti-revival forces, known as the "Old Lights," with a highly visible target for their attacks. To them he came to epitomize the anarchy and destruction of church harmony that the revival brought in its wake. The captain of these forces was Charles Chauncy (1705–1787), the co-pastor of Boston's prestigious First Church, who was also known as "Old Brick." Chauncy had first written of the revival in 1741, when he actually gave thanks for what the Spirit of God was doing. He had no doubt, he wrote, that there were "a number in this land, upon whom God has graciously shed the

---

6. For the public recantation that he made, see the excerpt from *Reverend Mr. James Davenport's Confession and Retractions* in *Great Awakening*, ed. Bushman, 53–55.

7. James Davenport, *The Faithful Minister Encouraged* (Philadelphia, PA: James Chattin, 1756), 9.

influence of this blessed Spirit," something for which he and his readers ought to be thankful. Yet he went on to note some concerns. There had arisen "unchristian heats and animosities" along with "rash, censorious, uncharitable judging." He said that "evil speaking, reviling and slandering" had become all too common.[8] Here, Chauncy clearly had in view the uncharitable way that men like Davenport often treated those whom they judged to be unconverted.

By the following year the prominent Boston pastor had become much more critical. In July of that year Davenport had appeared in Boston and specifically sought out Chauncy to pronounce judgment on the latter's spirituality. The encounter, which took place in the doorway of Chauncy's study, decisively turned the latter against the revival. He quickly fired off a sermon, published as *Enthusiasm Described and Cautioned Against*, in which he accused Davenport and his ilk of being "enthusiasts," that is, fanatics, who show their true colors by their blatant disregard of the "dictates of reason."[9] As a safeguard against their fanaticism, he first encouraged his hearers and readers to use the Scriptures—"the great rule of religion, the grand test in matters of salvation"—to test what was going on in New England. He also drew attention to the fact that "the Spirit of God deals with men as reasonable creatures." Reason, though not to be set up in place of God's revelation in the Bible, was essential to the Christian life. Failure to use it, as Davenport and his followers appeared to be doing, was a sure way to fall into "all manner of delusion."[10] In particular, Chauncy stressed that the arousal of one's "passions and affections" needs to be carefully monitored. The "passions," when properly acted upon by the Spirit, "tend mightily to awaken the reasonable powers." But if one's passions are set ablaze and one's reason

---

8. Cited in Taylor, "Spirit of the Awakening," 342–43.

9. A substantial portion of Chauncy's *Enthusiasm Described and Cautioned Against* may be conveniently found in Eugene E. White, *Puritan Rhetoric: The Issue of Emotion in Religion* (Carbondale, IL; Edwardsville, IL: Southern Illinois University Press, 1972), 103–16. For a good discussion of Chauncy's theological position, see Conrad Cherry, *The Theology of Jonathan Edwards: A Reappraisal* (1966, Bloomington, IN; Indianapolis: Indiana University Press, 1990), 164–67; Taylor, "Spirit of the Awakening," 335–70.

10. White, *Puritan Rhetoric*, 106, 112–13.

and understanding are not enlightened, it is all to no avail. Reason and judgment, the "more noble part" of the human being, must be preeminent in all religious experience, otherwise it is but a sham and "enthusiasm." Real religion, he concluded, is "a sober, calm, reasonable thing."[11]

Chauncy's main attack on the revival was his *Seasonable Thoughts on the State of Religion in New-England* (1743). It continued to press home what Chauncy saw as the main work of the Spirit, the enlightenment of the mind. "An enlightened mind, and not raised affections," he stated, "ought always to be the guide of those who call themselves men; and this, in the affairs of religion, as well as other things: And it will be so, where God really works on their hearts, by his Spirit."[12]

As the religious situation in New England began to polarize between those who took Chauncy's position and those who defended the revival, excesses and all, an Irish-born Presbyterian minister named John Moorehead (ca. 1703–1773), who was sympathetic to the revival, prayed: "God direct us what to do, particularly with pious zealots and cold, diabolical opposers!"[13] The answer to Moorehead's prayer came by way of a series of books from the pen of Edwards on the nature of true spirituality. In them, Edwards found himself in the unenviable position of giving an answer to both sides in the debate about the nature of the work of the Holy Spirit and what is a genuine revival. But this viselike situation brought forth one of the richest books on Christian spirituality in the history of the church, *A Treatise Concerning the Religious Affections* (1746). To the "pious zealots" like Davenport he stressed that biblical Christianity must involve the mind and reason. When God converts a person, light is shed upon the mind. On the other hand, there is much more to conversion than enlightenment. In response to Chauncy and those of his persuasion, he maintained that genuine spirituality flows out from a heart aflame

---

11. White, *Puritan Rhetoric*, 114–15. See also the discussion of this sermon by Taylor, "Spirit of the Awakening," 343–52.
12. Chauncy, *Seasonable Thoughts*, 327.
13. Cited in Goen, editor's introduction to *Great Awakening*, 64.

with the love of God. There is no genuine Christianity without a warm heart.

A Treatise Concerning the Religious Affections (1746)

Harold P. Simonson, who has written a book on Edwards as a theologian of the heart, has stated of Edwards's *Religious Affections* that it is the culmination of "some twenty-five years of thought about the nature of religious experience."[14] Iain Murray describes it as "one of the most important books possessed by the Christian church on the nature of true religion."[15] In it we find Edwards's most exhaustive and penetrating expositions of the nature of true Christian spirituality, a spirituality in which both heat and light are vital, and a spirituality that is rooted in Scripture. Edwards's *Religious Affections* seeks to answer the positions of both Davenport and Chauncy, but it is noteworthy that the longest section of the book is an answer to Davenport's position. Edwards regarded the misguided zeal of Davenport as a much more serious hindrance to the advance of the gospel in times of revival than the intellectualism of Chauncy.

The first section of the book argues against Chauncy that "true religion, in great part, consists in holy affections."[16] As Edwards notes, "The Holy Scriptures do everywhere place religion very much in the affections; such as fear, hope, love, hatred, desire, joy, sorrow, gratitude, compassion and zeal."[17] True faith is never found in a state of indifference to the things of God and Christ. Such a state is what the Scriptures call lukewarmness, which to God is revolting. At its heart, the Christian life is a Spirit-wrought passionate engagement of the entire person in living for Christ. In Edwards's words:

> The Spirit of God, in those that have sound and solid religion, is a spirit of powerful holy affection; and therefore, God is said to have given them the spirit of power, and of love, and of a sound mind (II Tim. 1:7). And such, when they receive the Spirit of God, in his

---

14. Harold P. Simonson, *Jonathan Edwards: Theologian of the Heart* (1974, Macon, GA: Mercer University Press, 1982), 56.
15. Murray, *Jonathan Edwards*, 267.
16. Edwards, *Religious Affections*, 95.
17. Edwards, *Religious Affections*, 102.

sanctifying and saving influences, are said to be baptized with the Holy Ghost, and with fire; by reason of the power and fervor of those exercises the Spirit of God excites in their hearts, whereby their hearts, when grace is in exercise, may be said to burn within them; as is said of the disciples (Luke 24:32).[18]

And as he declared in an ordination sermon preached on August 30, 1744:

> True grace is no dull, inactive, ineffectual principle; it is a powerful thing; there is an exceeding energy in it; and the reason is, that God is in it; it is a divine principle, a participation of the divine nature, and a communication of divine life, of the life of a risen Saviour, who exerts himself in the hearts of the saints, after the power of an endless life. They that have true grace in them, they live; but not by their own life; but Christ lives in them: his Holy Spirit becomes in them a living principle and spring of divine life: the energy and power of which is in Scripture compared to fire. Matt. iii. 11: "I indeed baptize you with water; but he that cometh after me is mightier than I, whose shoes I am not worthy to bear; he shall baptize you with the Holy Ghost, and with fire." True piety is not a thing remaining only in the head, or consisting in any speculative knowledge or opinions, or outward morality, or forms of religion; it reaches the heart, is chiefly seated there, and burns there. There is a holy ardor in every thing that belongs to true grace: true faith is an ardent thing.[19]

The Indwelling of the Spirit

After detailing what are not definite indications of the work of the Spirit, Edwards explores twelve signs of genuine Scriptural spirituality that are patent in times of revival. First, Edwards sees in passages like 1 Corinthians 3:16 and John 14:16–17 that the Holy Spirit indwells believers as His "proper lasting abode."[20] By means of this indwelling He imparts His character, which consists of holiness and godliness, to the Christian.[21] In other words, Edwards is convinced that genuine

---

18. Edwards, *Religious Affections*, 100.
19. Jonathan Edwards, *The True Excellency of a Gospel Minister* in *The Works of Jonathan Edwards* (1834, Edinburgh: Banner of Truth, 1974), 2:957.
20. Edwards, *Religious Affections*, 200.
21. Edwards, *Religious Affections*, 197–239.

Christian character is ultimately not a matter of human achievement. It has its root in the indwelling grace of the Holy Spirit. Genuine Christian spirituality begins with God.

It should be noted that Edwards regarded the indwelling of the Spirit as "the sum of the blessings Christ sought by what he did and suffered in the work of redemption." This comes from his book *An Humble Attempt to Promote Explicit Agreement and Visible Union of God's People in Extraordinary Prayer, For the Revival of Religion and the Advancement of Christ's Kingdom on Earth, pursuant to Scripture-Promises and Prophecies concerning the Last Time* (usually referred to simply as the *Humble Attempt*), published in 1748. As Edwards continued in this book: "The Holy Spirit, in his indwelling, his influences and fruits, is the sum of all grace, holiness, comfort and joy, or in one word, of all the spiritual good Christ purchased for men in this world: and is also the sum of all perfection, glory and eternal joy, that he purchased for them in another world."[22]

Loving God for Who He Is
Second, true love for God is based ultimately upon who He is in Himself and not on what He does for us. This second sign has been the subject of much discussion over the years since some readers have understood Edwards to be implying that self-love is totally excluded from the elect's relationship with God. This is not at all the case. Rather, Edwards was pressing home the fact that if their love for God were simply a loving of God for what He does on their behalf, namely saving them from the eternal horror of hell, then Christianity would simply be a subtle form of self-love. If people love God chiefly because of what He does for them, then, instead of God being the end of their existence, He becomes a means to an end, namely their happiness and self-fulfillment. But a biblical Christian loves God because He is altogether loveable and lovely.[23] Edwards did not rule out entirely ele-

---

22. Jonathan Edwards, *Humble Attempt* in his *Apocalyptic Writings*, ed. Stephen J. Stein, *The Works of Jonathan Edwards* (New Haven; London: Yale University Press, 1977), 5:341.
23. Edwards, *Religious Affections*, 240–53.

ments of self-love in a person's love for God.[24] But he rightly argued that love for God for who He is in Himself must ultimately be primary. Christianity that is real and possesses spiritual power is rooted in a love that does not seek its own advantage.

Then, this love for God for who He is in Himself is above all a love for God's holiness.[25] In the midst of his discussion of this third sign of genuine spirituality, Edwards made a truly important contribution to the history of Reformed thought. He stated that the Holy Spirit imparts to sinners at their conversion a new way of perceiving spiritual reality. This sense is more than simply an awareness of God and belief in God. It is nothing less than "a taste" for God's beauty and glory. In the words of the American historian John E. Smith, "A love of God which does not include the taste and relish of the divine beauty is not the love which reveals the saints."[26] From Edwards's perspective, the Christian, for example, does not merely rationally believe that God is glorious; he or she has a sense of the gloriousness of God in his or her heart.

Light and Conviction
One of Edwards's favorite statements was that genuine spiritual affections are "not heat without light."[27] The fourth sign of genuine Christianity is therefore a spiritually enlightened mind.[28] True Christians have a healthy respect for their minds and reason. Trust in the Scriptures as the supreme authority when it comes to truth and error does not entail, for Edwards, casting aside the use of one's mind.

Fifth, Edwards emphasized that genuine religious affections are accompanied by deep-seated conviction, "a solid, full, thorough and effectual conviction of the truth of the great things of the gospel."[29] For examples of such conviction, Edwards adduced a string of biblical examples, including Peter's confession of faith in Matthew 16:17, his

---

24. Edwards, *Religious Affections*, 246.
25. Edwards, *Religious Affections*, 253–66.
26. Smith, editor's introduction to *Religious Affections*, by Edwards, 30.
27. Edwards, *Religious Affections*, 266.
28. Edwards, *Religious Affections*, 266–91.
29. Edwards, *Religious Affections*, 291–311. The quote is from p. 291.

similar assertion in John 6:68–69, and Paul's confident assertion in 2 Corinthians 5:1, 6–8, regarding the life to come.[30]

Evangelical Humility

Edwards's sixth sign was that no affections are genuinely spiritual unless they are accompanied by what he calls "evangelical humiliation," what today we would call "evangelical humility."[31] By the term "evangelical humiliation" Edwards had in mind "a sense that a Christian has of his own utter insufficiency, despicableness, and odiousness, with an answerable frame of heart."[32] Edwards rightly saw spiritual pride as *the* major reason for serious blockage in the Christian life. In a letter that Edwards wrote to Deborah Hatheway (1722–1753), an eighteen-year-old Christian from Suffield, Massachusetts, when she asked for advice on how to live the Christian life, he told her:

> Remember that pride is the worst viper that is in the heart, the greatest disturber of the soul's peace and sweet communion with Christ. It was the first sin that ever was, and lies lowest in the foundation of Satan's whole building. It is the most difficult to root out, and it is the most hidden, secret, and deceitful of all lust, and it often creeps in, insensibly, into the midst of religion and sometimes under the disguise of humility.[33]

Having had long experience in unravelling the labyrinth of the human heart, Edwards was very aware of how deeply self-righteousness and self-exaltation are wedded to the faculty of the human heart. And it is precisely the person who is anxious to be a vital Christian, in contrast to those who seem lifeless and indifferent, who is most at risk to falling prey to spiritual pride. It is the zealous who are prone to comparing themselves with others so that they appear in a good and glorious light.[34] Genuine spirituality, though, sees its own poverty and its need for grace and for God. The person "whose heart is under the power

---

30. Edwards, *Religious Affections*, 292–93.
31. Edwards, *Religious Affections*, 311–40.
32. Edwards, *Religious Affections*, 311.
33. Edwards, *Advice to Young Converts* in *Edwards' Resolutions and Advice*, ed. Nichols, 32.
34. Edwards, *Religious Affections*, 320–40.

of Christian humility…is apt to think his attainments in religion to be comparatively mean, and to esteem himself low among the saints, and one of the least of saints."[35] A mark of true spirituality is thus the renunciation of the personal desire for glory. The truly awakened heart is not one that rests in its own spiritual attainments or great spiritual experiences. Rather, with loving acknowledgement and self-abandon, it rests in the glory of God and of His Son.

This was true to Scripture—among other texts, Edwards refers to Psalm 34:18; 51:17; and Isaiah 66:1–2[36]—and attested by Edwards's own experience. As he once wrote in a document never intended for public consumption:

> I have often since I lived in this town [that is, Northampton], had very affecting views of my own sinfulness and vileness; very frequently so as to hold me in a kind of loud weeping, sometimes for a considerable time together; so that I have often been forced to shut myself up. I have had a vastly greater sense of my own wickedness, and the badness of my heart, since my conversion, than ever I had before. It has often appeared to me, that if God should mark iniquity against me, I should appear the very worst of all mankind; of all that have been since the beginning of the world to this time: and that I should have by far the lowest place in hell…. And it appears to me, that were it not for free grace, exalted and raised up to the infinite height of all the fullness and glory of the great Jehovah, and the arm of his power and grace stretched forth, in all the majesty of his power, and in all the glory of his sovereignty; I should appear sunk down in my sins infinitely below hell itself, far beyond sight of everything, but the piercing eye of God's grace, that can pierce even down to such a depth, and to the bottom of such an abyss.[37]

Rooted in Conversion

The seventh sign is very similar to the first: authentic Christian spirituality has its roots in conversion.[38] Truly gracious affections depend totally upon this radical event that turns sinners toward God

---

35. Edwards, *Religious Affections*, 320.
36. Edwards, *Religious Affections*, 312–13.
37. Edwards, *Personal Narrative* in his *Letters and Personal Writings*, ed. Claghorn, *Works of Jonathan Edwards*, 16:801–2.
38. Edwards, *Religious Affections*, 340–44.

and away from their corrupt nature and changes their goals, motivations, and outlook on life. In discussing this topic of conversion, it is noteworthy that Edwards did not touch on that which evangelicals in more recent days have tended to focus on: "the exact moment" when an individual is saved. Like his Puritan forebears, Edwards was more concerned about discerning whether this great change has taken place or not than dating it.[39]

Moreover, Edwards stressed that conversion does not bring immediate perfection.[40] Past patterns of sinning and sinful inclinations do not all totally disappear, but their dominion is now broken, for the very reason that these sinful patterns now stand in relationship to a new self, which, in virtue of its permanent place in the believer's life, must reveal itself over the course of time. "Conversion," Edwards wrote, "don't entirely root out…those sins which a man by his natural constitution was most inclined to before his conversion." But "it is of great power and efficacy…to correct" them.[41] Edwards thus wanted to stress that genuine spirituality not only has its roots in a new nature, but in an *abiding* new nature.

Christlike Gentleness and Christian Tenderness
Edwards's eighth sign was that where there has been a genuine conversion, it is accompanied by a Christlike character, "the lamblike, dovelike spirit and temper of Jesus Christ."[42] This does not mean that boldness for Christ or Christian zeal are wrong per se and that Christian spirituality is wimpish. But Edwards was concerned that sometimes "a pretended boldness for Christ…arises from no better principle than pride" and that zeal for Christ can be marked by "bitterness against the persons of men."[43] Christian boldness and zeal are "indeed a flame, but a sweet one."[44]

---

39. Smith, editor's introduction to *Religious Affections*, by Edwards, 37.
40. Edwards, *Religious Affections*, 341–42.
41. Edwards, *Religious Affections*, 341.
42. Edwards, *Religious Affections*, 344–57. The quote is from page 344.
43. Edwards, *Religious Affections*, 352, 353.
44. Edwards, *Religious Affections*, 352.

He instanced Christ in his fiercest battle against the forces of darkness, namely at the cross and in the events leading up to it. What temper marked him then, he asked. His holy boldness and valor were not shown in "fierce and violent speeches," displaying "sharp and bitter passions." On the contrary, there was an "all-conquering patience," as well as love and prayer for his enemies: "never did he appear so much a Lamb, and never did he show so much of the dovelike spirit, as at that time."[45]

"Like a Burnt Child That Dreads the Fire"

Ninth, Christians have a tender heart, especially toward God. They are sensitive to all that displeases Him.[46] They are "like a burnt child that dreads the fire."[47] They are very conscious of how sin separates them from the God they love, and so they strive not to readmit it to their lives and press on to be as godlike in behavior and conduct as they can.

Such tenderness of conscience, Edwards affirmed, is the only proper attitude for one trying to respond to the heart-work of the Spirit. Referring to verses like Psalm 2:11 and Psalm 147:11, Edwards maintained that while the believer no longer fears hell, he or she is increasingly fearful of causing God pain by indulging in sin. There is a "diminishing of the fear of hell, with an increase of the fear of sin." Such a believer "has the firmest comfort, but the softest heart."[48]

Consistency and Constancy

The next sign dealt with the aesthetic side of the Christian life. Edwards never tired of emphasizing that God's holiness is beautiful in the most profound sense of that term. This beauty is expressed by the harmony and balance in the life of the believer.[49] Where there is true piety, there is balance. Why is this so? There is balance because the Spirit of Christ, who is the source of all genuine Christian affections,

---

45. Edwards, *Religious Affections*, 351.
46. Edwards, *Religious Affections*, 357–64.
47. Edwards, *Religious Affections*, 364.
48. Edwards, *Religious Affections*, 364.
49. Edwards, *Religious Affections*, 365–76.

now indwells them. It is the Holy Spirit who brings this balance. Moreover, the Holy Spirit is transforming the believer into the image of God, who is Himself beauty and harmony. So one can rightly expect that Christians would reflect this in their own personhood.

Hypocrites, on the other hand, are bound to reveal a disharmony and disproportion in their affections. In some of them there is "the most confident hope, while they are void of reverence, self-jealousy and caution." While "many hypocrites rejoice without trembling," in the saints "joy and holy fear go together."[50]

Here Edwards was being critical of those whose religion consists of what he called "fits and starts," who are committed only at certain seasons, or who focus on this or that virtue to the neglect of all else.[51] Such men and women fail to exhibit the symmetry that is the shape of true spirituality. Edwards compared them to "waters in the time of a shower of rain, which during the shower, and a little after, run like a brook and flow abundantly, but are presently quite dry." The true saint, on the other hand, is "like a stream from a living spring; which, though it may be greatly increased by a shower of rain, and diminished in time of drought, yet constantly runs."[52]

"A Holy Breathing and Panting"

Edwards's eleventh sign was that a truly Christian spirituality is marked by a longing for more of God.[53] He tied this sign closely with one he had enumerated earlier in the treatise, namely that of evangelical humility. The more grace believers receive, "the more they see their imperfection and emptiness, and distance from what ought to be."[54] Marked by a consciousness of how far they have yet to go in the Christian life, true believers long after God for more of Him. For proof, Edwards turned to Paul's words in Philippians 3:13–15 and declared: "the greatest eminence and perfection, that the saints arrive

---

50. Edwards, *Religious Affections*, 366.
51. Edwards, *Religious Affections*, 372.
52. Edwards, *Religious Affections*, 373.
53. Edwards, *Religious Affections*, 376–83.
54. Edwards, *Religious Affections*, 378.

at in this world, has no tendency to satiety, or to abate their desires after more; but on the contrary, makes 'em more eager to press forwards" and know more of God.[55]

Moreover, Edwards emphasized that the more persons have of holy affections, the more they have of that spiritual taste for God's beauty and glory that he had mentioned earlier in his discussion of the third sign. Edwards wrote: "Spiritual good is of a satisfying nature; and for that very reason, the soul that tastes, and knows its nature, will thirst after it, and a fullness of it, that it may be satisfied. And the more he experiences, and the more he knows this excellent, unparalleled, exquisite, and satisfying sweetness, the more earnestly will he hunger and thirst for more, till he comes to perfection."[56] As Edwards put it in a remarkable turn of phrase, there is in the true believer "a holy breathing and panting after the Spirit of God, to increase holiness."[57]

The Acid Test—The Fruit of the Spirit

To the twelfth and final sign Edwards devoted more space than to any of the others, a fact that indicates that it loomed largest in his mind. True spirituality bears visible fruit in Christian practice and living in the world.[58] And this practice has three major characteristics. First, it is shaped by what Edwards called "Christian rules," that is "the laws of Christ, laws that he and his apostles did abundantly insist on, as of the greatest importance and necessity."[59] Second, the living of the Christian life is the believer's main business in this world. As Edwards noted with regard to Titus 2:14: Christ's people "not only do good works, but are zealous of good works."[60] Third, genuine Christian spirituality has in it the crucial quality of perseverance. The real believer makes Christianity his main business not only on Sundays, or at certain extraordinary seasons, but that "business which he perseveres in

---

55. Edwards, *Religious Affections*, 377.
56. Edwards, *Religious Affections*, 379.
57. Edwards, *Religious Affections*, 382.
58. Edwards, *Religious Affections*, 383–461.
59. Edwards, *Religious Affections*, 387.
60. Edwards, *Religious Affections*, 387.

through all changes, and under all trials, as long as he lives."[61] In other words, while works do not save us, we cannot be saved without them. "Obedience, good works, good fruits, are to be taken…as a sure evidence to our own consciences of a true principle of grace."[62]

The Humble Attempt (1748)

One final work of Edwards related to the subject of revival that should be taken note of is his *Humble Attempt*, which appeared in January 1748. In this work Edwards made a stirring appeal for "many people, in different parts of the world, by express agreement to come into a visible union in extraordinary, speedy, fervent and constant prayer, for those great effusions of the Holy Spirit, which shall bring on that advancement of Christ's church and kingdom, that God has so often promised shall be in the latter ages of the world."[63] Edwards was thoroughly convinced, and rightly so, on the basis of Scripture and the history of the church, that "when God has something very great to accomplish for his church, it is his will that there should precede it the extraordinary prayers of his people."[64]

Unlike some of his other works, this book did not have a great impact in Edwards's own lifetime. Toward the end of the eighteenth century, though, it exercised a profound influence, especially on a circle of Particular Baptists in the English Midlands, which we shall look at in the chapters to follow.[65]

---

61. Edwards, *Religious Affections*, 383–84.
62. Edwards, *Religious Affections*, 424.
63. Edwards, *Humble Attempt* in his *Apocalyptic Writings*, ed. Stein, 320.
64. Edwards, *Some Thoughts Concerning the Present Revival of Religion in New England* in *Great Awakening*, ed. Goen, 516.
65. For the influence of Edwards's *Humble Attempt* on this group of English Baptists see below, chap. 9.

CHAPTER 7

"We Are a Garden Wall'd Around"
Particular Baptists Needing Revival

Enclosed gardens were a common feature in the towns and villages of seventeenth- and early eighteenth-century England. While some of these gardens were developed for aesthetic reasons and consisted primarily of flowers and shrubs, many of them were kitchen gardens, designed to produce small fruits, herbs, salad greens and other vegetables. Generally rectangular in shape, they were enclosed by walls, fences or hedges that might reach as high as sixteen feet. These walls provided both protection from the elements and privacy for the owner.[1] In fact, during the turbulent era of the 1640s, when the British Isles experienced the horrors and ravage of civil war, such gardens came to be increasingly seen as "places of secure retreat from the dangers of political and religious strife."[2]

It was during this very era that the Particular Baptists appeared on the English church scene. Reformed in their soteriology, congregationalist in church government, and espousing believer's baptism, they grew from seven congregations in London in 1644 to roughly one hundred and thirty in 1660. By 1689, there may well have been close to three hundred across the British archipelago. The growth from 1660 to 1689 is particularly striking since it was during this period that a series of laws were passed, known as the Clarendon Code, which

---

1. Helen M. Leach, "Kitchen Garden" in *The Oxford Companion to Gardens*, ed. Geoffrey Jellicoe *et al.*, (Oxford; New York: Oxford University Press, 1986), 314–15; Geoffrey Jellicoe, "Walled Garden" in his ed., *The Oxford Companion to Gardens*, 592–93; David C. Stuart, *Georgian Gardens* (London: Robert Hale Ltd., 1979), 142–43.

2. Tom Turner, *English Garden Design: History and Styles Since 1650* (Woodbridge, Suffolk: Antique Collectors' Club Ltd., 1986), 9.

made it illegal to worship in any other setting but that of the established church and which basically reduced any but Church of England members to second-class citizens. From 1660 to 1688 the Baptists, along with other groups outside of the Church of England, were thus hurled into the fierce fire of persecution. Baptists who refused to go along with these laws often ended up experiencing state harassment, paying substantial fines, or experiencing life-threatening imprisonment.

Now, the confessional document that underlay much of the growth in the first fifty or so years of the Particular Baptist denomination is the First London Confession of Faith (1644). The articles dealing with the church in this confession draw heavily, as one would expect, upon the Scriptures. On occasion, however, the document also has recourse to ideas and images redolent of the world of mid-seventeenth-century England. One of these images is that of the enclosed garden. According to article XXXIV of this statement of faith, by entering the local church through the doorway of baptism, believers are placing themselves under Christ's "heavenly conduct and government, to lead their lives in his walled sheep-fold, and watered garden."[3] This description of the church as a "watered garden" is drawn from the Song of Solomon 4:12: "A garden inclosed is my sister, my spouse; a spring shut up, a fountain sealed." But in the minds of the first readers of this statement it would also recall the enclosed gardens of seventeenth-century English horticulture and impress upon their minds that their churches were meant to be havens of order, refreshment, and fruitfulness, sanctuaries from the chaos and wilderness of the world.

Over the next century this image of the "garden enclosed" would recur again and again in Calvinistic Baptist documents that talked about the nature of the church. Benjamin Keach, for example, could maintain:

> God hath out of the people of this world, taken his churches and walled them about, that none of the evil beasts can hurt them: all mankind naturally were alike dry and barren, as a wilderness, and

---

3. William L. Lumpkin, *Baptist Confessions of Faith*, rev. ed. (Valley Forge, PA: Judson Press, 1969), 165–66.

brought forth no good fruit. But God hath separated some of this barren ground, to make lovely gardens for himself to walk and delight in.... The church of Christ, is a garden enclosed, or a community of Christians distinct from the world: "A garden enclosed is my sister, my spouse" Cant. iv.12.[4]

The covenant of Bourton-on-the-Water Baptist Church, Gloucestershire, drawn up in 1719/1720, to cite another instance, stated that members of the church must "promise to keep the secrets of our Church entire without divulging them to any that are not members of this particular body, tho' they may be otherwise dear & near to us; for we believe the Church ought to be as a garden enclosed & a fountain sealed."[5] And to step outside of the Calvinistic Baptist community for a moment, the hymn of Isaac Watts has as its first stanza:

> We are a garden wall'd around,
> Chosen and made peculiar ground;
> A little spot enclos'd by grace
> Out of the world's wide wilderness.[6]

This image of an enclosed garden, though, had about it an inevitable air of insularity. It could easily become a picture of refusal to engage with what was outside the garden. So it was that far too many sectors of the Calvinistic Baptist community in the eighteenth century were inward-looking and insular, closeting themselves within their meetinghouses and limiting their horizons to the maintenance of church life. The image of the "enclosed garden" which had been such a positive image in the seventeenth century became a picture of stagnation in the following century.

During the eighteenth century, however, a revolution occurred in gardening. The enclosed garden of the seventeenth century gave way to wide, expansive lawns with manmade lakes and groves designed

---

4. Keach, *Gospel Mysteries Unveiled*, 2:332, 339.

5. Charles W. Deweese, *Baptist Church Covenants* (Nashville, TN: Broadman Press, 1990), 124. For a similar use of this image, see Benjamin Keach, *The Glory of a True Church, and Its Discipline Display'd* (London, 1697), 50–51.

6. Isaac Watts, *Hymns and Spiritual Songs*, book I, hymn 74 in *The Works of the Reverend and Learned Isaac Watts, D.D.*, comp. George Burder (London: John Barfield, 1810), 4:274.

by professional gardeners like Lancelot Brown (1715–1783), otherwise known as "Capability Brown." The shift well fit the temper of the eighteenth century: optimistic, forward-looking, eager to explore the world. A similar transformation occurred in many of the sectors of the eighteenth-century English Particular Baptist community that had known spiritual stagnation and even decline. Fueled by a recommitment to fervent evangelism in the last quarter of the eighteenth century, their focus shifted from parochial concerns to the vistas of the wider world. It should be emphasized, though, that there were areas of the English Particular Baptist community that remained spiritually healthy throughout this period, and we want to look at them toward the close of this chapter.

Declension among the Particular Baptists

After thirty years almost of state persecution, religious toleration came with the coup d'état that overthrew James II (1633–1701) in 1688, and the Baptists were now free to plant and build congregations, though it was still illegal for them to evangelize outside of their church buildings. Yet, despite the advent of toleration, the denomination as a whole began to plateau in its growth and in some parts of England actually went into decline. In 1715 there were around 220 Calvinistic Baptist churches in England and Wales. By 1750 that number had declined to about 150.[7] As Daniel Turner (1710–1798), pastor of Abingdon Baptist Church, wrote in 1769 to his friend, Samuel Stennett (1727–1795), a Particular Baptist pastor in London:

> The Baptist Denomination... in my opinion is upon the decline. Useful solid ministers are taken away, & few likely to fill up their places. Many churches are destitute. Useful learning is rather discouraged

---

7. For these figures, see W. T. Whitley, "The Baptist Interest under George I," *Transactions of the Baptist Historical Society* 2 (1910–1911): 95–109; Arthur S. Langley, "Baptist Ministers in England about 1750 A.D.," *Transactions of the Baptist Historical Society* 6 (1918–1919): 138–57; Alan D. Gilbert, *Religion and Society in Industrial England: Church, Chapel and Social Change, 1740–1914* (London; New York: Longman Group Ltd., 1976), 35, 37; Watts, *The Dissenters*, 267–71, 491–510.

amongst us. A confident assurance goes farther with many, even well-meaning people, than good sense, learning and piety.[8]

Andrew Fuller (1754–1815), whose revival ministry we shall look at in detail in the next chapter, used much stronger language to depict this declension. Drawing his imagery from the farmyard, a world with which he was very familiar, Fuller noted in the mid-1790s that if many of these stagnant Baptist causes had not been shaken out of their lethargy, the Particular Baptist cause would have soon "been a very dunghill in society!"[9]

Various reasons can be cited for this declension. It would not be surprising that after expending enormous energy in resisting state persecution from 1660 to 1688, even to the point of death in the case of a few pastors and elders, some of the Baptist congregations were simply burnt out spiritually and mentally unable to engage in aggressive evangelism.[10] Then, it bears remembering that it was illegal for Baptists or any other Nonconformist groups to engage in mass evangelism outside of their meetinghouses. Money and effort thus began to be poured into the erection of church buildings instead of evangelistic outreach.[11] Moreover, prior to the erection of a meetinghouse, services might be held at a variety of geographical locations and thus a congregation could have an impact over a wide area. But once the building went up, members who lived at a distance were expected to make their way to the meetinghouse, and thus the impact in the various locations was somewhat diminished. So it was that the monetary value of the property of the Particular Baptists increased, but its membership was beginning to decrease.[12]

---

8. O. C. Robison, "The Particular Baptists in England, 1760–1820" (PhD thesis, Regent's Park College, Oxford University, 1963), 173–74.

9. Andrew Fuller, "Discipline of the English and Scottish Baptist Churches" in *Complete Works of the Rev. Andrew Fuller*, 3:478.

10. I am deeply thankful to Pastor Ken Hart of Cradley Chapel, Cradley, Worcestershire, who reminded me of this at the 2010 Revival Conference of the Wales Evangelical School of Theology.

11. Paul Langford, *A Polite and Commercial People: England 1727–1783* (Oxford: Clarendon Press, 1989), 257.

12. W. T. Whitley, *A History of British Baptists*, 2nd ed. (London: The Kingsgate Press, 1932), 215–16.

Then there was the development of the theological position known as High Calvinism, sometimes called Hyper-Calvinism. Pastors and believers of this persuasion were rightly convinced that salvation is God's work from start to finish. On the basis of this conviction, however, they erroneously reasoned that since unbelievers are unable to turn to Christ, it was therefore unscriptural to urge them to come to the Savior. Genuinely desirous of exalting God's sovereignty in salvation, High Calvinist preachers shied away from calling all and sundry to repentance and faith, lest any of the credit for the salvation of sinners go to them. God, in His own time, would convert the elect and bring them into the "enclosed gardens" of the Particular Baptist community.

Andrew Fuller (1754–1815), for instance, whose role in the revival of the Particular Baptists we will look at in more detail in the next chapter, was raised in a Baptist work in the small village of Soham, not far from the university town of Cambridge. Its pastor was John Eve (d. 1782), who ministered at Soham from 1752 till his resignation in 1771. Eve was a typical High Calvinist. His preaching, as Fuller later recalled, "was not adapted to awaken [the] conscience," and he "had little or nothing to say to the unconverted."[13] Thus, even though Fuller regularly attended the Baptist meetinghouse with his family, he gave little heed or thought to the sermons that he heard. Nevertheless, and despite his own experience, Fuller found himself preaching much like Eve during the early years of his pastoral ministry. "Encumbered" with inhibitions, he could not bring himself to offer the gospel indiscriminately to sinners.[14]

Response to the Evangelical Revival

Now, it is vital to note that while many Baptists were in this state of declension, from the mid-1730s onwards, as we have seen, there was a tremendous movement of revival going on in Great Britain. The Spirit

---

13. Cited in John Ryland, *The Work of Faith, the Labour of Love, and the Patience of Hope, Illustrated; in the Life and Death of the Rev. Andrew Fuller*, 2nd ed. (London: Button & Son, 1818), 12.

14. Andrew Fuller, *The Gospel Worthy of All Acceptation* (*Works*, 2:329).

of God was moving powerfully throughout British society on both sides of the Atlantic, and tens of thousands of men and women were shaken out of their spiritual slumber and death, drawn irresistibly to adore and to serve the Lord Christ. Many Particular Baptists, however, had deep reservations about the revival. The Wesleys, of course, were Arminians and thus beyond the pale for these *Calvinistic* Baptists. Furthermore, the Wesleys' view of the Baptists was hardly conducive to good relations. Here is Charles Wesley in 1756 speaking about the Baptists in his diary. In his words they were "a carnal…contentious sect, always watching to steal away our children, and make them as dead as themselves."[15] However, Whitefield was a Calvinist. Yet the fervency of his evangelism and his urging of the lost to embrace Christ, their only hope of salvation, prompted several Particular Baptist critics to complain of what they termed his "Arminian accent."

Most importantly, these Baptists were disturbed by the fact that the earliest leaders in the revival belonged to the Church of England. Their Baptist forebears, after all, had come out of the Church of England at great personal cost and suffering, and they had suffered for their determination to establish true gospel churches. The heritage that came down to the eighteenth-century Particular Baptists was thus intertwined with a great concern for proper New Testament church order. Though writing early in the century, Benjamin Keach expresses the ecclesiological convictions that prevailed in the Particular Baptist community for much of the eighteenth century. In his commentary on the parables of Jesus, Keach unequivocally states vis-à-vis Ezekiel 34:14 that this text implies that God's people

> shall wander no more on the mountains of error and heresy; Christ leads them out of all idolatry and superstition, out of Babylon and all false worship; they shall no more be defiled with women, that is, by the pollution of false churches, or with harlot worship; the church of Rome is called the mother of harlots. Are there no false churches but the Romish church? Yea, there are, no doubt; she hath whorish daughters, though not such vile and beastly harlots as the mother is; all churches that sprang from her, or all of the like

---

15. Cited in John R. Tyson, ed., *Charles Wesley: A Reader* (New York; Oxford: Oxford University Press, 1989), 418.

nature, in respect of their constitution, and that retain many of her superstitious names, garbs, rites, and ceremonies, no doubt they are her daughters. Were the gospel churches national, or did they receive into those churches profane persons? No, no, they were a separate people, and a congregational and a holy community, being not conformable to this world; and into such a church Jesus Christ brings his sheep. And from hence it followeth, that he carries his lost sheep when he hath found them into his own fold, or into some true gospel church.[16]

Later in the eighteenth century this position was reiterated by the man who was the leading Particular Baptist divine for much of that century, John Gill (1697–1771). In a pamphlet that Gill had published in 1751 for fellow Baptists in Wales to use specifically in reply to Welsh Anglicans, Gill declared in no uncertain terms: the Church of England is not "a true church of Christ" for she is not congregational in polity, which was "the form and order of…the first Christian churches," and the doctrine preached in her pulpits is "very corrupt, and not agreeable to the word of God."[17] Similarly William Herbert (1697–1745), a Welsh Baptist pastor and a friend of Howel Harris, was critical of the latter's decision to stay in the Church of England. In a letter that he wrote to Harris early in 1737, a couple of years after the Evangelical Revival had begun in England and Wales, Herbert likened the Church of England to a pub "which is open to all comers" and to a "common field where every noisesome beast may come." Surely Harris realized, Herbert continued, that the Scriptures—and he had in mind the Song of Solomon 4:12—describe God's church as "a garden enclosed, a spring shut up, a fountain sealed," in other words, a body of believers "separate from the profane world"?[18] From Herbert's point of view, Harris's commitment to an apostate institution put a serious question mark upon the latter's entire ministry. A

---

16. Keach, *Gospel Mysteries Unveiled*, 2:383.

17. John Gill, *The Dissenters Reasons for Separating from the Church of England* (London: G. Keith, 1751), 102, 104. Gill's pamphlet proved to be fairly popular, going through four editions in less than ten years.

18. D. D. J. Morgan, "The Development of the Baptist Movement in Wales between 1714 and 1815 with Particular Reference to the Evangelical Revival" (unpublished DPhil thesis, University of Oxford, 1986), 39–40.

resolution passed by St. Mary's Baptist Church, Norwich, in 1754 also reveals this attitude. In the minute book for that year we read that "it is unlawful for any…to attend the meetings of the Methodists, or to join in any worship which is contrary to the doctrines and ordinances of our Lord Jesus."[19] Many eighteenth-century Particular Baptists were thus adamant in their refusal to regard the Evangelical Revival as a genuine work of God for, from their perspective, it simply did not issue in "true gospel churches."

Of course, as we shall see at the close of this chapter, there were some noteworthy exceptions, but up until the 1770s far too many Particular Baptists seem to have assumed that a revival could only be considered genuine if it preserved and promoted the proper form of the local church. For many Particular Baptists of the first six or seven decades of the eighteenth century, outward form and inward revival went hand in hand. Their chief preoccupation was the preservation of what they considered the proper New Testament form of church. In their minds, when God brought revival it would have to issue in true gospel churches like theirs.[20]

The dilemma facing these Particular Baptists was not an easy one. They rightly felt constrained to emphasize the New Testament idea of the local church as a congregation of visible saints and assert that the concept of a state church is antithetical to the whole tenor of the new covenant. Moreover, these were truths for which their forebears in the previous century had suffered much. To abandon them would have been unthinkable. But what then was to be made of the ministry of men like Whitefield? One possible solution would have been for the eighteenth-century Particular Baptists to have viewed the ministry of Whitefield and other Anglican Calvinists in the way that their seventeenth-century forebears viewed the labors of the sixteenth-century Reformers. The latter did not reject the ministry of the Reformers because they were not Baptists. Rather,

---

19. Cited in Charles B. Jewson, "St. Mary's, Norwich," *The Baptist Quarterly* 10 (1940–1941): 283.

20. R. Philip Roberts, *Continuity and Change: London Calvinistic Baptists and The Evangelical Revival 1760–1820* (Wheaton, IL: Richard Owen Roberts Publishers, 1989), 81.

they recognized that the Reformers had been greatly used by God to bring the church out of the stygian darkness of the Middle Ages. Yet, though the Reformers did well, the Baptists reckoned that they had failed to apply all that the Scriptures taught. As Benjamin Keach said about the Particular Baptist community's recovery of certain key New Testament principles:

> Why will not our brethren keep to the great institution, and exact rule of the primitive church? Must we content our selves with the light which the Church had in respect of this and other Gospel-truths at the beginning of the Reformation,—since God hath brought forth greater (to the praise of his own rich grace) in our days?[21]

Similarly, it could have been recognized that God was indeed at work among the leaders of the revival, but that there were certain areas—in particular, those dealing with the church and its nature—where they needed greater light.

Some Examples of Spiritual Vitality

Yet there are instances of sterling spiritual vitality in this period.[22] One thinks of the unremitting ardor of William Mitchel (1662-1705) and David Crosley (1669-1744), who, between 1688 and 1705, evangelized towns and villages throughout east Lancashire and the West Riding of Yorkshire from their base at Bacup in the Rossendale Valley.[23] In so doing, they laid the foundations for a large number of future Baptist churches. Then there is what was called the Western Association, those churches in the West Country, which includes the historic

---

21. Cited in James M. Renihan, "The Puritan Roots of Reformed Baptists" (unpublished paper, March 12, 1998), 24.

22. Helpful in writing portions of this section has been James M. Renihan, "A Tale of Two Associations" (unpublished paper, March, 1997).

23. For further details, see W. E. Blomfield, "Yorkshire Baptist Churches in the 17th and 18th Centuries" in *The Baptists of Yorkshire*, 2nd ed. (Bradford; London: Wm Byles & Sons Ltd.; London: Kingsgate Press, 1912), 73-88; Ian Sellers, ed., *Our Heritage: The Baptists of Yorkshire, Lancashire and Cheshire* (Leeds: The Yorkshire Baptist Association; The Lancashire and Cheshire Baptist Association, 1987), 10-11; B. A. Ramsbottom, *The Puritan Samson: The Life of David Crosley 1669-1744* (Harpenden, Hertfordshire: Gospel Standard Trust Publications, 1991).

counties of Cornwall, Devon, Dorset, and Somerset. Though they were not without their ups and downs, their zeal for the gospel, evangelical Calvinism, revival, and the visible extension of Christ's kingdom was unflagging. In 1718–1719, for example, when a great controversy over subscribing to a Trinitarian creed arose among the Nonconformist churches in Exeter and then later was vociferously debated at Salter's Hall in London, the Western Association asserted the importance of churches subscribing to a confessional statement. Fourteen years later, in 1733, they did this very thing when they renewed their commitment to the Second London of Confession of Faith (1677/1689), which had replaced the First London Confession of Faith as the doctrinal standard of the Particular Baptists. They subsequently kept up fellowship with one another through the yearly printing of an association letter, a practice later adopted by other Baptist associations.

It was in the geographical heart of this association, at Bristol, that the first Baptist school for training pastors was organized, the Bristol Baptist Academy. It was initially funded by a generous bequest from the will of Edward Terrill (1635–1686), an elder in the Broadmead Church, Bristol. The roll call of alumni from the Academy is impressive, a good number of whom played a role in the revival of the Particular Baptist churches.[24] As British Baptist historian Raymond Brown has noted:

> Many of…[the] Bristol students brought an outstanding contribution to the life of the churches in the second half of the eighteenth century. Men like John Ash (1724–79) of Pershore, Benjamin Beddome (1717–95) of Bourton-on-the-Water and Benjamin Francis of Horsley were content to serve their respective churches for between forty and fifty years, pouring their entire working ministry into the pastoral care of rural congregations, faithful biblical preaching, the development of association life, the establishment of new causes and, in each case, the composition or publication of hymns. Their devotional hymnology, passion for associating, and evangelistic initiatives helped to divert many churches from high Calvinism and

---

24. For details, see Roger Hayden, *Continuity and Change: Evangelical Calvinism among Eighteenth-Century Baptist Ministers Trained at Bristol Academy, 1690–1791* (Milton under Wychwood, Chipping Norton, Oxfordshire: Nigel Lynn Publishing for Roger Hayden and the Baptist Historical Society, 2006).

introduced them to these influences which were powerfully at work in the Evangelical Revival.[25]

Let us look more closely at one of these men that Brown mentions, namely, Benjamin Francis (1734–99).[26]

A year after leaving Bristol Baptist Academy in 1756, Benjamin Francis was called to the Baptist work at Horsley, Gloucestershire. When he came there the membership consisted of sixty-six people. When he died forty-two years later, close to 450 had been converted under his ministry in the church, baptized, and brought into membership. The meetinghouse was enlarged three times during Francis's ministry, so that by the early nineteenth century the church was one of the largest in the English Particular Baptist community. Francis attributed much of the success that attended his preaching to the Sunday prayer meetings the church held at six o'clock in the morning and in the afternoon before the afternoon service. Fifty or sixty would come to the Sunday morning prayer meeting, while at the afternoon prayer meeting the vestry would literally overflow with people.[27]

His preaching, though, was not only heard at Horsley. In the biographical sketch of Francis that his son-in-law Thomas Flint (d. 1819) drew up within a few weeks of Francis's death, we are told that:

> He was the first means of introducing evangelical religion into many dark towns and villages in all the neighbourhood round [Horsley]. For many years he made excursions monthly into the most uninstructed parts of Gloucestershire, Worcestershire and

---

25. Raymond Brown, *The English Baptists of the Eighteenth Century* (London: The Baptist Historical Society, 1986), 84–85.

26. For the life of Francis, the following sources have been extremely helpful: Thomas Flint, "A Brief Narrative of the Life and Death of the Rev. Benjamin Francis, A.M.," annexed to John Ryland, Jr., *The Presence of Christ the Source of Eternal Bliss. A Funeral Discourse,… occasioned by the Death of the Rev. Benjamin Francis, A.M.* (Bristol, 1800), 33–76; Geoffrey F. Nuttall, "Questions and Answers: An Eighteenth-Century Correspondence," *The Baptist Quarterly* 27 (1977–1978): 83–90; Geoffrey F. Nuttall, "Letters by Benjamin Francis", *Trafodion* (1983), 4–8. I have also benefited from Gwyn Davies, "A Welsh Exile: Benjamin Francis (1734–99)" (unpublished manuscript, 1999), 3 pages. There is a portrait of Francis in John Rippon, ed., *The Baptist Annual Register*, 2 (1794–1797), opposite p. 327.

27. "A List of the Particular Baptist Churches in England, 1798" in John Rippon, ed., *The Baptist Annual Register* 3 (1798–1801): 14–15.

Wiltshire; besides visiting his brethren, and strengthening their hands in God. In the course of his route through Worcestershire, which he regularly attended from about 1772 to 1784, it appears he had preached in Cheltenham 130 Sermons, at Tewkesbury 136, at Pershore 137, and at Upton upon Severn 180: his manner was to set out from home on Monday morning, and return on Friday evening, after taking a circuit of 90 miles, and preaching every evening. In Wiltshire, on the other side of Horsley, he established a monthly lecture at Malmesbury which he supplied from 1771 to 1799, so that he preached there 282 sermons, and for the latter part of the time he reached as far as Christian-Malford where he had preached 84 Sermons. He extended his journey frequently as far as Devizes, 30 miles from home, where he preached 56 times, and oftener to Melksham, Frome, Trowbridge, and Bradford at each of which four places he had preached 90 Sermons. At Wotton-under-edge, seven miles from Horsley, he kept up a monthly lecture for thirty years, and preached there 394 times. At Uley, five miles distant, he maintained another stated lecture for many years, and had preached 350 Sermons there.[28]

In addition to these extensive labors, Francis also regularly preached in places as far away as London and Dublin, Portsmouth and Plymouth, as well as undertaking repeated preaching tours of his native Wales. In a day when travel to a town but twenty miles away was a significant undertaking,[29] this record of Francis's itinerant ministry is positively amazing and parallels the sort of itinerancy that characterizes the evangelical revivals in the Church of England.

One gets a good idea of the piety of Francis from the following quotes. Writing in October 1796, to his close friend, Daniel Turner, he said:

> O that my thoughts and affections were more as a well of living water, rising as high as the throne of God and the Lamb! What shall I do with this vain roving heart, which is my daily burden? When shall heaven prevail over earth, and bear away all the pollutions of

---

28. Flint, "Brief Narrative," 45–46. The names of the towns and villages referred to by Flint have been modernized according to current spelling.

29. See the informative discussion of travel in this period and the following century by Sven Birkerts, *The Gutenberg Elegies: The Fate of Reading in an Electronic Age* (New York, NY: Fawcett Columbine, 1994), 24–25.

my corrupt nature? I often think, whatever opinions others may entertain of me, that I am in myself a chaos of ignorance and a mass of deformity. I need the Holy Spirit to enlighten me, and the blood of Christ to cleanse me, and a lively faith in the atoning Lamb, now as much as ever.[30]

And in a letter to another friend dated November 6, 1798, he declared:

> O that every sacrifice I offer were consumed with the fire of ardent love to Jesus. Reading, praying, studying and preaching are to me very cold exercises, if not warmed with the love of Christ. This, this is the quintessence of holiness, of happiness, of heaven. While many professors desire to know that Christ loves them, may it ever be my desire to know that I love him, by feeling his love mortifying in me the love of self, animating my whole soul to serve him, and, if called by his providence, to suffer even death for his sake.[31]

This Christ-centeredness that permeates these writings of Francis is the very atmosphere of the revival that comes to Baptist ranks, as we shall see.

Anne Steele

But what of the Baptist believer in the pew? If we had time, we could enumerate several examples of vital piety. We must content ourselves with one—Anne Steele (1717–1778).[32] Anne was the daughter of William Steele (1689–1769), the pastor of the Particular Baptist chapel in Broughton, Hampshire, a village situated roughly midway between Salisbury and Winchester. Converted in 1732 and baptized the same year, she grew to be a woman of deep piety, genuine cheerfulness, and

---

30. Cited in Flint, "Brief Narrative," 56–57.
31. Cited in Flint, "Brief Narrative," 58–59.
32. For Anne Steele, see Karen Smith, "The Community and the Believers: A Study of Calvinistic Baptist Spirituality in Some Towns and Villages of Hampshire and the Borders of Wiltshire, c. 1730–1830" (DPhil dissertation, University of Oxford, 1986); J. R. Broome, *A Bruised Reed: The Life and Times of Anne Steele* (Harpenden, Hertfordshire: Gospel Standard Trust Publications, 2007); Nancy Jiwon Cho, "'The Ministry of Song': Unmarried British Women's Hymn Writing, 1760–1936" (PhD thesis, Durham University, 2007), 43–84; Cynthia Y. Aalders, *To Express the Ineffable: The Hymns and Spirituality of Anne Steele* (Milton Keynes; Colorado Springs; Hyderabad: Paternoster, 2008); and Priscilla Chan, "Anne Steele's Spiritual Vision: Seeing God in the Peaks, Valleys and Plateaus of Life" (MTS thesis, Toronto Baptist Seminary, 2010).

with a mind hungry for knowledge. Her piety was wrought in the furnace of affliction. She wrestled most of her adult life, it appears, with ongoing bouts of tertian malaria and terrible stomach pain. Anne was unmarried and thus had the time to devote herself to hymn writing, a gift that the Lord had richly blessed her with. After her death, her hymns were as well known in evangelical circles as those of Isaac Watts, for instance.

One of the very few of her hymns that is still sung today reveals the way in which this wide circulation of her hymns would have played a part in revitalizing areas of the Particular Baptist cause throughout England. It was originally entitled "The Savior's Invitation," and was based on Jesus's words in John 7:37, "If any man thirst, let him come unto me, and drink":

> The Saviour calls—let every Ear
> Attend the heavenly Sound;
> Ye doubting Souls, dismiss your Fear,
> Hope smiles reviving round.
>
> For every thirsty, longing Heart,
> Here Streams of Bounty flow,
> And Life, and Health, and Bliss impart,
> To banish mortal Woe.
>
> Here, Springs of sacred Pleasure rise
> To ease your every Pain,
> (Immortal Fountain! full Supplies!)
> Nor shall you thirst in vain.
>
> Ye Sinners come, 'tis Mercy's Voice,
> The gracious Call obey;
> Mercy invites to heavenly Joys,—
> And can you yet delay?
>
> Dear Savior, draw reluctant Hearts,
> To Thee let Sinners fly;
> And take the Bliss Thy Love imparts,
> And drink, and never die.[33]

Based on Jesus's open invitation to sinners to come to Him and drink, that is, find eternal life, Steele urged "every Ear" to "attend"

---

33. Anne Steele, *A Collection of Hymns Adapted to Public Worship*, 3rd ed. (Bristol: W. Pine, 1778), hymn 145.

to Christ's heavenly invitation. He calls all who are "thirsty" and "longing" to come to him, where they will find "Life, and Health, and Bliss," in sum, "Springs of sacred Pleasure" that will ease every woe. This invitation is a command—"the gracious Call obey"—and a free offer—"can you yet delay?"[34] But Steele was also aware that the "thirsty, longing Heart" is not sufficient in itself to come to Christ. In the final analysis it is a "reluctant Heart," filled with doubt and fear. Hence, she prayed, "Dear Savior, draw reluctant hearts." And this is a prayer that can be prayed with confidence, for the Savior to whom she speaks is an "Immortal Fountain," mercy incarnate who loves sinners and delights in bestowing on them "heavenly joys." As Baptist men and women of England sang such hymns, God was preparing them for the "reviving" that we are about to consider in the next chapters.

---

34. On the free offer of the gospel in Steele's hymns, see further Sharon James, *In Trouble and in Joy: Four Women Who Lived for God* (Darlington, England: Evangelical Press, 2003), 154.

CHAPTER 8

"Impress Thy Truth upon My Heart with Thine Own Seal"
Andrew Fuller and Theological Reformation

The English Baptists did not emerge from their spiritual "winter" until the last two or three decades of the eighteenth century. And just as there were a variety of reasons for their decline, so there were a variety of reasons for their revival. Most notably, there was theological reformation, in which the High Calvinism of the past was largely rejected in favor of a truly evangelical Calvinism. *The Gospel Worthy of All Acceptation*, written by Andrew Fuller and first published in 1785, was the book that crystallized this movement of theological renewal.[1] Though forgotten in many Baptist circles, Andrew Fuller was once described by Charles Haddon Spurgeon (1834–1892) as "the greatest theologian" of his century.[2] And the Southern Baptist historian A. H. Newman (1852–1933) once commented that Fuller's "influence on American Baptists" was "incalculable" for good.[3] More recently, Gordon Rupp has referred to Fuller as the "mainspring" behind the impact of the evangelical revival on the English Particular Baptists.[4]

Fuller wrote major theological works on a variety of issues, many of them in the area of apologetics. For instance, he wrote refutations of such eighteenth-century theological aberrations as Socinianism and Sandemanianism, and in 1799 published the

---

1. For a study of Fuller as a theologian, see Phil Roberts, "Andrew Fuller" in Timothy George and David S. Dockery, eds., *Theologians of the Baptist Tradition* (Nashville, TN: Broadman & Holman, 2001), 34–51.

2. Cited in Gilbert Laws, *Andrew Fuller, Pastor, Theologian, Ropeholder* (London: Carey Press, 1942), 127.

3. Albert H. Newman, "Fuller, Andrew" in *The New Schaff-Herzog Encyclopedia of Religious Knowledge*, ed. Samuel Macauley Jackson (repr., Grand Rapids: Baker, 1963), 4:409.

4. Gordon Rupp, *Religion in England 1688–1791* (Oxford: Clarendon Press, 1986), 487.

definitive eighteenth-century Baptist response to Deism.[5] But it was through his rebuttal of High Calvinism that he made his most distinctive contribution to the revival of the English Particular Baptists. As Phil Roberts, formerly President of Midwestern Baptist Theological Seminary, has noted in a study of Fuller as a theologian:

> [Fuller] helped to link the earlier Baptists, whose chief concern was the establishment of ideal New Testament congregations, with those in the nineteenth century driven to make the gospel known worldwide. His contribution helped to guarantee that many of the leading Baptists of the 1800s would typify fervent evangelism and world missions.... Without his courage and doctrinal integrity in the face of what he considered to be theological aberrations, the Baptist mission movement might have been stillborn.[6]

Pathway to Conversion

The youngest of three brothers, Andrew Fuller was born on February 6, 1754, at Wicken, a small village now on the edge of the Cambridgeshire Fens, about six miles from the cathedral city of Ely. His parents, Robert Fuller (1723–1781) and Philippa Gunton (1726–1816), rented and worked a succession of dairy farms.[7] Baptists by conviction, both of them came from a Dissenting background, of which there were various congregations in the area. When Fuller was seven years of age, his family moved to the village of Soham, about two and a half miles

---

5. Fuller's main refutation of Socinianism may be found in *The Calvinistic and Socinian Systems Examined and Compared, as to Their Moral Tendency* in *The Complete Works of the Rev. Andrew Fuller*, rev. by Joseph Belcher, 3rd London ed. (1845, Harrisonburg, VA: Sprinkle Publications, 1988), 2:108–242. Further references to this edition of Fuller's works will cite it as simply *Works*. For Fuller's reply to Sandemanianism, see *Strictures on Sandemanianism, in Twelve Letters to a Friend* (*Works*, 2:561–646). His chief response to Deism, especially that of the popularizer Thomas Paine (1737–1809), is *The Gospel Its Own Witness* (*Works*, 2:1–107).

For examinations of Fuller's reply to these theological aberrations, see Michael A. G. Haykin, "'The Oracles of God': Andrew Fuller and the Scriptures," *Churchman* 103 (1989): 60–76; Michael A. G. Haykin, "A Socinian and Calvinist Compared: Joseph Priestley and Andrew Fuller on the Propriety of Prayer to Christ," *Dutch Review of Church History* 73 (1993): 178–98; Thomas Jacob South, "The Response of Andrew Fuller to the Sandemanian View of Saving Faith" (ThD thesis, Mid-America Baptist Theological Seminary, 1993).

6. Roberts, "Andrew Fuller," 132–33.

7. Andrew Gunton Fuller, "Memoir" (*Works*, 1:1).

from Wicken. Once settled in Soham, they joined themselves to the Particular Baptist work in the village that met for worship in a rented barn.[8] The pastor of the work was a certain John Eve (d. 1782), originally a sieve-maker from Chesterton, near the town of Cambridge. Eve had been set apart to preach the gospel by St. Andrew's Street Baptist Church, Cambridge, in 1749,[9] and three years later he was ordained as the first pastor of the Baptist cause at Soham, where he ministered for nearly twenty years till his resignation in 1771.

Fuller later remarked that Eve was a High Calvinist or, as he put it, one whose teaching was "tinged with false Calvinism."[10] As such, Eve did not believe that it was the duty of the unregenerate to exercise faith in Christ. To be sure, they could be urged to attend to outward duties such as hearing God's Word preached or being encouraged to read the Scriptures, but nothing of a spiritual nature could be required of them since they were dead in sin and only the Spirit could make them alive to spiritual things.[11] Eve's sermons, Fuller thus noted, were "not adapted to awaken [the] conscience" and "had little or nothing to say to the unconverted."[12]

When he was fourteen, though, Fuller began to entertain thoughts about the meaning and purpose of life. He was much affected by passages that he read from the biography of John Bunyan (1628–1688), his *Grace Abounding to the Chief of Sinners*, as well as Bunyan's *Pilgrim's Progress* and some of the works of Ralph Erskine (1685–1752), the Scottish evangelical and Presbyterian minister. These affections

---

8. [Ted Wilson], *Soham Baptist Church 250th Anniversary 1752–2002* ([Soham]: [Soham Baptist Church], 2002), [1]. This is an 8-pg. stapled pamphlet without pagination.

9. L. G. Champion, L. E. Addicott, and K. A. C. Parsons, *Church Book: St Andrew's Street Baptist Church, Cambridge 1720–1832* (London: Baptist Historical Society, 1991), 17.

10. Andrew Fuller, Letter to Charles Stuart, 1798, in Michael A. G. Haykin, *The Armies of the Lamb: The Spirituality of Andrew Fuller* (Dundas, ON: Joshua Press, 2001), 59. In 1798, Fuller wrote two long letters to Charles Stuart (1745–1826) about his early years. They are reproduced in Haykin, *Armies of the Lamb*, 59–74. For an overview of the history of High Calvinism in this period, see Peter Toon, *The Emergence of Hyper-Calvinism in English Nonconformity, 1689–1765* (London: Olive Tree, 1967).

11. Fuller, "Memoir" (*Works*, 1:12).

12. Fuller, "Memoir" (*Works*, 1:2).

were often accompanied by weeping and tears, but they ultimately proved to be transient, there being no radical change of heart.

Now, a popular expression of eighteenth-century Particular Baptist spirituality was the notion that if a scriptural text forcefully impressed itself upon one's mind, it was to be regarded as a promise from God. One particular day in 1767 Fuller had such an experience. Romans 6:14 ("sin shall not have dominion over you; for ye are not under the law, but under grace") came with such suddenness and force that Fuller naively believed that God was telling him that he was in a state of salvation and no longer under the tyranny of sin. But that evening, he later recalled, "I returned to my former vices with as eager a gust as ever."[13]

For the next six months he utterly neglected prayer and was as wedded to his sins as he had been before this experience. When in the course of 1768 he once again seriously reflected upon his lifestyle, he was conscious that he was still held fast in thralldom to sin. What then of his experience with Romans 6:14? Fuller refused to doubt that it was given to him as an indication of his standing with God. He was, he therefore concluded, a converted person, but backslidden. He still lived, though, with never a victory over sin and its temptations, and with a total neglect of prayer. "The great deep of my heart's depravity had not yet been broken up," he later commented about these experiences of his mid-teens.[14]

In autumn of 1769 he once again came under the conviction that his life was displeasing to God. He could no longer pretend that he was only backslidden. "The fire and brimstone of the bottomless pit seemed to burn within my bosom," he later declared. "I saw that God would be perfectly just in sending me to hell, and that to hell I must go, unless I were saved of mere grace." Fuller now recognized the way that he had sorely abused God's mercy. He had presumed that he was a converted individual, but all the time he had had no love for God and no desire for His presence, no hunger to be like Christ and no love for His people. On the other hand, he could not bear,

---

13. Fuller, letter to Charles Stuart, in Haykin, *Armies of the Lamb*, 62–63.
14. Fuller, letter to Charles Stuart, in Haykin, *Armies of the Lamb*, 63–64.

he said, "the thought of plunging myself into endless ruin." It was at this point that Job's resolution—"though he slay me, yet will I trust in him" (Job 13:15)—came to mind, and Fuller grew determined to cast himself upon the mercy of the Lord Jesus "to be both pardoned and purified."[15]

Yet, the High Calvinism that formed the air that he had breathed since his earliest years proved to be a real barrier to his coming to Christ. It maintained, as we have seen, that in order to flee to Christ for salvation, the "warrant" that a person needed to believe that he or she would be accepted by Christ was a subjective one. Conviction of one's sinfulness and deep mental anguish as a result of that conviction were popularly regarded by hyper-Calvinists as such a warrant. From this point of view, these experiences were signs that God was in the process of converting the individual that was going through them. The net effect of this teaching was to place the essence of conversion and faith not in believing the gospel, "but in a persuasion of our being interested in its benefits." Instead of attention being directed away from oneself toward Christ, the convicted sinner was turned inwards upon himself or herself to search for evidence that he or she was being converted.[16] Against this perspective Fuller would later argue that the gospel exhortation to believe in Christ was a sufficient enough warrant to come to the Lord Jesus.

Fuller was in the throes of a genuine conversion and quite aware of his status as a sinner, but under the influence of the High Calvinist spirituality of conversion, he was convinced he had neither the qualifications nor the proper warrant to flee to Christ in order to escape the righteous judgment of God. Upon later reflection he saw his situation as akin to that of Queen Esther. She went into the presence of her husband, the Persian King Ahasuerus, at the risk of her life since it was contrary to Persian law to enter the monarch's presence uninvited. Similarly, Fuller decided: "I will trust my soul, my sinful, lost

---

15. Fuller, letter to Charles Stuart, in Haykin, *Armies of the Lamb*, 69–71.
16. Fuller, *Strictures on Sandemanianism* (*Works*, 2:563–64). See also E. F. Clipsham, "Andrew Fuller and Fullerism: A Study in Evangelical Calvinism," *The Baptist Quarterly* 20 (1963–1964): 103.

soul in his [that is, Christ's] hands—if I perish, I perish!" So it was in November of 1769 that Fuller found peace with God and rest for his troubled soul in the cross of Christ.[17]

His personal experience prior to and during his conversion ultimately taught him three things in particular. First, there was the error of maintaining that only those sinners aware of and distressed about their state have a warrant or right to come to Christ. Second, genuine faith is Christ-centered, not a curving inward upon oneself to see if there was any desire to know Christ and embrace His salvation. Third, he recognized that true conversion is rooted in a radical change of the affections of the heart and manifest in a lifestyle that seeks to honor God.[18]

The following spring, 1770, Fuller was baptized and joined the church at Soham. Within six years the church had called Fuller to be their pastor. Now, though he had personally known the deadening effect of hyper-Calvinistic preaching, Fuller knew no other way of dealing with non-Christians from the pulpit and initially, he said, he "durst not…address an invitation to the unconverted to come to Jesus."[19] But as he studied the style of preaching exhibited in the Acts of the Apostles and especially in Christ's ministry, he began to see that "the Scriptures abounded with exhortations and invitations to sinners." But how was this style of preaching to be reconciled with the biblical emphasis on salvation being a sovereign work of grace?[20]

By 1780 Fuller had come to see clearly that his own way of preaching was unduly hampered by a concern not to urge spiritual duties upon non-believers. As he wrote in his diary for August 30 of that year:

> Surely Peter and Paul never felt such scruples in their addresses as we do. They addressed their hearers as *men*—fallen men; as we should warn and admonish persons who were blind and on the brink of some dreadful precipice. Their work seemed plain before them. Oh that mine might be so before me![21]

---

17. Fuller, letter to Charles Stuart, in Haykin, *Armies of the Lamb*, 71–72.
18. Clipsham, "Andrew Fuller and Fullerism," 106–7.
19. Fuller, "Memoir" (*Works*, 1:12).
20. Fuller, "Memoir" (*Works*, 1:15).
21. Fuller, "Memoir" (*Works*, 1:23).

The "pulpit," Fuller commented a few months later,

> seems an awful place!—An opportunity for addressing a company of immortals on their eternal interests—Oh how important! We preach for eternity. We in a sense are set for the rising and falling of many in Israel.... Oh would the Lord the Spirit lead me into the nature and importance of the work of the ministry![22]

And by the time that Fuller left Soham to take up the pastorate of the Baptist work in Kettering, Northamptonshire, he was convinced, as he told the Kettering congregation at his induction on October 7, 1783, that

> it is the duty of every minister of Christ plainly and faithfully to preach the gospel to all who will hear it. And, as I believe the inability of men to spiritual things to be wholly of the moral, and therefore of the criminal kind—and that it is their duty to love the Lord Jesus Christ and trust in him for salvation, though they do not—I, therefore, believe free and solemn addresses, invitations, calls, and warnings to them, to be not only consistent, but directly adapted, as means in the hands of the Spirit of God to bring them to Christ. I consider it as a part of my duty, which I could not omit without being guilty of the blood of souls.[23]

This theological revolution in Fuller's sentiments about the duty of sinners to believe the gospel and how that gospel should be preached were later encapsulated in a book, *The Gospel of Christ Worthy of All Acceptation* (1785), and in his lifetime his views came to be known as Fullerism. As Geoffrey F. Nuttall once observed, Fuller is thus one of the few Englishmen to have a theological perspective named after him and it "points to a remarkable achievement."[24] Two editions of *The Gospel of Christ Worthy of All Acceptation* were issued in Fuller's lifetime. A first draft had been written by 1778, the manuscript of which was purchased by The Southern Baptist Theological Seminary a number of years ago. It begins thus:

---

22. Fuller, "Memoir" (*Works*, 1:25), diary entries for February 5 and 8, 1781.

23. Andrew Fuller, *Confession of Faith* XV, in Haykin, *Armies of the Lamb*, 279.

24. Geoffrey F, Nuttall, "Northamptonshire and The Modern Question: A Turning-point in Eighteenth-Century Dissent" in his *Studies in English Dissent* (Weston Rhyn, Oswestry, Shropshire: Quinta Press, 2002), 205.

What a narrow path is truth! How many extremes are there into which we are liable to run! Some deny truth; others hold it, but in unrighteousness. O Lord, impress thy truth upon my heart with thine own Seal, then shall I receive it as in itself it is, "A doctrine according to godliness."[25]

This draft was eventually rewritten and published as the first edition in Northampton in early 1785. It bore a lengthy subtitle: *The Obligations of Men Fully to Credit, and Cordially to Approve, Whatever God Makes Known, Wherein is Considered the Nature of Faith in Christ, and the Duty of Those Where the Gospel Comes in That Matter*. A second edition appeared in 1801 with a simplified title and subtitle, *The Gospel Worthy of All Acceptation: The Duty of Sinners to Believe in Jesus Christ*, which expressed the overall theme of both editions of the book.[26] There were a number of substantial differences between the two editions, which Fuller freely admitted and which primarily related to the doctrine of particular redemption, but the major theme remained unaltered: "faith in Christ is the duty of all men who hear, or have opportunity to hear, the gospel."[27] Or as he put it in his preface to the first edition: "true faith is nothing more nor less than an hearty or cordial belief of what God says, surely it must be every one's duty where the gospel is published, to do that. Surely no man ought to question or treat with indifference any thing which Jehovah hath said."[28]

---

25. Andrew Fuller, "Thoughts on the Power of Men to do the Will of God" [1777/1778] (Ms., Archives, James P. Boyce Centennial Library, The Southern Baptist Theological Seminary), 1.

26. For the second edition, see *Works*, 2:328–416. For studies of this work, see Clipsham, "Andrew Fuller and Fullerism," 214–25; James E. Tull, *Shapers of Baptist Thought* (Valley Forge, PA: Judson Press, 1972; Macon, GA: Mercer University Press, 1984), 85–92; Peter J. Morden, *Offering Christ to the World: Andrew Fuller (1754–1815) and the Revival of Eighteenth Century Particular Baptist Life*, Studies in Baptist History and Thought (Carlisle: Paternoster, 2003), 8:23–76.

27. Andrew Fuller, *The Gospel Worthy of All Acceptation* (*Works*, 2:343). Extremely helpful in tracing the differences between the two editions is Robert W. Oliver, *History of the English Calvinistic Baptists 1771–1892: From John Gill to C. H. Spurgeon* (Edinburgh: Banner of Truth, 2006), 156–72.

28. Andrew Fuller, preface to *The Gospel of Christ Worthy of All Acceptation*, 1st ed. (Northampton, [1785]), iv. Subsequent references to this work are to the first edition unless otherwise noted.

What is quickly evident in both editions is the large amount of space given to closely reasoned exegesis.

In the first edition, for example, Fuller devotes the second major part of the work to showing that "faith in Christ is commanded in the Scriptures to unconverted sinners."[29] It had been reflection on Psalm 2, for instance, that had first led Fuller to doubt the Hyper-Calvinist refusal to countenance faith as the duty of the unconverted.[30] He now undertook an interpretation of this text in light of his subject, reading it, as the New Testament reads it in Acts 4, as a messianic psalm. The command to "the heathen" and "the people" of Israel (v. 1) as well as to "the kings of the earth" and "the rulers" (v. 2)—interpreted in Acts 4:27 as "Herod, and Pontius Pilate, with the Gentiles, and the people of Israel"—to "kiss the Son" (v. 12) is a command given to those "who were most certainly enemies to Christ, unregenerate sinners." And "kissing the Son" Fuller understood to be "a spiritual act," which from the perspective of the New Testament meant nothing less than "being reconciled to, and embracing the Son of God, which doubtless is of the very essence of true saving faith."[31] Clearly, Fuller reasoned, here was both Old and New Testament support for his position.

A number of Johannine texts, however, plainly revealed that "true saving faith" is "enjoined [by the New Testament] upon unregenerate sinners."[32] John 12:36, for instance, contains an exhortation of the Lord Jesus to a crowd of men and women to "believe in the light" that they might be the children of light. Working from the context, Fuller argued that Jesus was urging His hearers to put their faith in Him. He is the "light" in whom faith is to be placed, that faith which issues in salvation (John 12:46). Those whom Christ commanded to exercise such faith, however, were rank unbelievers of whom it is said earlier "they believed not on him" (John 12:37) and, in fact, Fuller pointed out on the basis of the quote of Isaiah 6:10 in John 12:40, "it seems"

---

29. Fuller, *Gospel of Christ*, 37.
30. Fuller, *Gospel of Christ*, iii.
31. Fuller, *Gospel of Christ*, 37–39.
32. Fuller, *Gospel of Christ*, 40.

that these very same people whom Christ called to faith in Him "were given over to judicial blindness, and were finally lost."[33]

Then there is John 6:29, where Jesus declares to sinners that "this is the work of God, that ye believe on him whom he hath sent." Fuller pointed out that this statement is made to men who in the context are described as following Christ simply because He gave them food to eat (v. 26) and who are considered by Christ to be unbelievers (v. 36). Christ rebukes them for their mercenary motives and urges them to "labour not for the meat which perisheth, but for that meat which endureth unto everlasting life" (v. 27). Their response as recorded in verse 28 is to ask Christ, "What shall we do, that we might work the works of God?" His answer is to urge them to put their faith in him (v. 29). It is as if, Fuller said, Christ had told them, faith in him is "the first duty incumbent" upon them "without which it will be impossible…to please God."[34]

Again, in John 5:23 Fuller read that all men and women are to "honour the Son, even as they honour the Father." Giving honor to the Son entails, Fuller reasoned, "holy hearty love to him" and adoration of every aspect of His person. It necessarily "includes faith in him." Christ has made Himself known as a supreme monarch, an advocate who pleads the cause of His people, a physician who offers health to the spiritually sick, and an infallible teacher. Therefore, honoring Him in these various aspects of His ministry requires faith and trust.[35]

Among the practical conclusions that followed from such Scriptural argumentation was that preachers of the gospel must passionately exhort their hearers to repent and commit themselves to Christ.[36] In the second edition, Fuller sharpened this emphasis, for he was more than ever convinced that there was "scarcely a minister amongst us"—that is, amongst the Particular Baptist denomination—"whose preaching has not been more or less influenced by the lethargic systems of the age."[37] Far too many of Fuller's fellow Baptist ministers

---

33. Fuller, *Gospel of Christ*, 40.
34. Fuller, *Gospel of Christ*, 40–43.
35. Fuller, *Gospel of Christ*, 43–44.
36. Fuller, *Gospel of Christ*, 163–72.
37. Fuller, *Gospel Worthy of All Acceptation* (*Works*, 2:387).

failed to imitate the preaching of Christ and the apostles who used to exhort the unconverted to immediate repentance and faith. For a variety of reasons, they regarded the unconverted in their congregations as "poor, impotent…creatures." Faith was beyond such men and women and could not be pressed upon them as an immediate, present duty. Fuller was convinced that this way of conducting a pulpit ministry was unbiblical and simply helped the unconverted to remain in their sin.[38] Without a doubt, Fuller's conclusion that ministers needed to press home repentance and faith as immediate duties upon all of their hearers was foundational to later argument by William Carey that this needed to take place not only in England but throughout the world.[39]

There is a direct line from the publication of the *Gospel of Christ Worthy of All Acceptation* to Fuller's wholehearted involvement in the formation of the Particular Baptist Society for the Propagation of the Gospel among the Heathen in 1792—later known as the Baptist Missionary Society and which sent Carey to India in 1793—and Fuller's subsequent service as secretary of that society until his death in 1815. The work of the mission consumed an enormous amount of Fuller's time as he regularly toured the country, representing the mission and raising funds. On average he was away from home three months of the year. Between 1798 and 1813, for instance, he made five lengthy trips to Scotland for the mission as well as undertaking journeys to Wales and Ireland.[40] Consider one of these trips, that made to Scotland in 1805. In less than sixty days Fuller travelled thirteen hundred miles and preached fifty sermons for the cause of the Baptist mission. He also carried on an extensive correspondence both to the missionaries on the field and to supporters at home. Finally, he supervised the selection of missionary appointees and sought to deal with troubles

---

38. Fuller, *Gospel Worthy of All Acceptation* (*Works*, 2:387–93).

39. In Harry R. Boer's words: "Fuller's insistence on the duty of all men everywhere to believe the gospel…played a determinative role in the crystallization of Carey's missionary vision," *Pentecost and Missions* (Grand Rapids: Eerdmans, 1961), 24. See also Brian Stanley, *The History of the Baptist Missionary Society 1792-1992* (Edinburgh: T&T Clark, 1992), 12–13.

40. On Fuller's trips to Scotland, see Dudley Reeves, "Andrew Fuller in Scotland," *The Banner of Truth* 106-7 (July/August 1972): 33–40; Michael A. G. Haykin, "Andrew Fuller and His Scottish Friends," *History Scotland*, 15, no. 6 (November/December 2015): 24–30.

as they emerged on the field. In short, he acted as the pastor of the missionaries sent out.[41]

As he poured himself into the work of the Baptist Missionary Society, Fuller continued to refine his thinking about missions. Along with his rethinking of the responsibility of both preachers and hearers of the gospel discussed above, there emerged a fresh perspective on the nature of the church. There is little doubt that Fuller wholly affirmed traditional Particular Baptist thinking about the church. In that tradition the church is a body of people who have personally repented, exercised faith in Christ, and borne witness to this inner transformation by baptism.[42] But Fuller was also concerned to emphasize something else about the church.

When Fuller spoke of the local church after he had assumed the role of secretary of the mission his emphasis often fell on the church's responsibility to evangelize and indeed participate in taking the gospel to the ends of the earth. As he wrote, for example, in 1806:

> The primitive churches were not mere assemblies of men who agreed to meet together once or twice a week, and to subscribe for the support of an accomplished man who should on those occasions deliver lectures on religion. They were men gathered out of the world by the preaching of the cross, and formed into society for the promotion of Christ's kingdom in their own souls and in the world around them. It was not the concern of the ministers or elders only; the body of the people were interested in all that was done, and, according to their several abilities and stations, took part in it. Neither were they assemblies of heady, high-minded, contentious people, meeting together to argue on points of doctrine or discipline, and converting the worship of God into scenes of strife. They spoke the truth; but it was in love: they observed discipline; but, like an army of chosen men, it was that they might attack the kingdom of Satan to greater advantage. Happy were it for our churches if we could come to a closer imitation of this model![43]

---

41. Doyle L. Young, "Andrew Fuller and the Modern Mission Movement," *Baptist History and Heritage* 17 (1982): 17–27.

42. See in this regard Michael A. G. Haykin, "'Hazarding All for God at a Clap': The Spirituality of Baptism among British Calvinistic Baptists," *The Baptist Quarterly* 38 (1999–2000): 185–95.

43. Andrew Fuller, *The Pastor's Address to His Christian Hearers, Entreating their Assistance in Promoting the Interest of Christ* (*Works*, 3:346).

Fuller certainly had no wish to abandon either the stress on doctrinal preaching for the edification of God's people or that on proper discipline, but he had rightly noted that the pursuit of these concerns to the exclusion of evangelism had produced in all too many eighteenth-century Particular Baptist churches contention, bitter strife, and endless disputes. These inward-looking concerns had to be balanced with an outward focus on the extension of Christ's kingdom.

Moreover, evangelism was not simply to be regarded as the work of only "the ministers or elders." The entire body of God's people were to be involved. This conception of the church is well summed up in another text, which, like the one cited above, compares the church of Christ to an army. "The true churches of Jesus Christ," he wrote five years before his death, "travail in birth for the salvation of men. They are the armies of the Lamb, the grand object of whose existence is to extend the Redeemer's kingdom."[44] Retaining the basic structure of earlier Baptist thinking about the church, Fuller added one critical ingredient drawn from his reading about the life of the church in the New Testament: the vital need for local Baptist churches to be centers of vigorous mission and evangelism.

Fuller's thought about the preaching of the gospel was critical in the revival of the Particular Baptist churches in Britain, as we shall see. Not only that. It pushed them into ardent evangelism and mission, which, in turn, was a critical step in the global expansion of the gospel. Fuller's experience also reveals that when the Spirit comes with His reviving power, He always comes as the Spirit of truth and brings a measure of theological renewal. The Reformation, for instance, is often regarded simply as a time of significant theological renewal. Yet, it was also a time of revival. The revival of the Particular Baptists at the close of the eighteenth century was, of course, a time of revival. But there was also theological reformation involved, in this case, the breaking of the power of High Calvinism in the Particular Baptist community.

---

44. Andrew Fuller, *The Promise of the Spirit, the Grand Encouragement in Promoting the Gospel* (*Works*, 3:359).

Calls for Repentance

Along with Fuller's rethinking the nature of conversion and the preaching of the gospel, he made calls for repentance. For instance, in Fuller's *Causes of Declension in Religion, and Means of Revival*, a tract that he wrote in 1785, Fuller outlined the spiritual apathy then reigning among many Baptists of his day.

> It is to be feared the old puritanical way of devoting ourselves wholly to be the Lord's, resigning up our bodies, souls, gifts, time, property, with all we have and are to serve him, and frequently renewing these covenants before him, is now awfully neglected. This was to make a business of religion, a life's work, and not merely an accidental affair, occurring but now and then, and what must be attended to only when we can spare time from other arrangements. Few seem to aim, pray, and strive after eminent love to God and one other. Many appear to be contented if they can but remember the time when they had such love in exercise, and then, tacking to it the notion of perseverance without the thing, they go on and on, satisfied, it seems, if they do but make shift just to get to heaven at last, without much caring how. If we were in a proper spirit, the question with us would not so much be What must I do for God? as, What can I do for God? A servant that heartily loves his master counts it a privilege to be employed by him, yea, an honour to be entrusted with any of his concerns.[45]

Many, Fuller noted, were merely content to get to "heaven without concerning themselves overly about *how* they get there." The practice of giving oneself wholly to God that had been common among the seventeenth-century Puritans had generally ceased to be part of the Christian lives of late eighteenth-century Baptists. This apathy was well revealed in the question, "What must I do for God?" In other words, they were asking, "What is the minimum I must do to get to heaven?" Seeking to change this dire situation, Fuller suggested:

> If it is required "What then is to be done? Wherein in particular can we glorify God more than we have done?", we answer by asking: Is there no room for amendment? Have we been sufficiently earnest and constant in private prayer? Are there none of us that have

---

45. Andrew Fuller, *Causes of Declension in Religion, and Means of Revival* (*Works*, 3:320).

> opportunities to set apart particular times to pray for the effusion of the Holy Spirit? Can we do more than we have done in instructing our families? Are there none of our dependents, workmen, or neighbours that we might speak to, at least so far as to ask them to go and hear the gospel? Can we rectify nothing in our tempers and behaviour in the world so as better to recommend religion? Cannot we watch more? Cannot we save a little more of our substance to give to the poor? In a word, is there no room or possibility left for our being more meek, loving, and resembling the blessed Jesus than we have been?
>
> To glorify God, and to recommend by our example the religion of the meek and lowly Jesus, are the chief ends for which it is worth while to live; but do we sufficiently pursue these ends?[46]

Here, Fuller listed five ways in which his fellow Baptists could prepare themselves for renewal: prayer; the cultivation of Christianity in the home; sharing the gospel with unbelievers; an honest examination of what needs to be changed in one's character and purposefully seeking to change it, especially when it comes to love and meekness; and finally, the development of a spirit of generosity to those in need. At the close of the tract Fuller returned to the importance of prayer for revival:

> Finally, brethren, let us not forget to intermingle prayer with all we do. Our need of God's Holy Spirit to enable us to do any thing, and every thing, truly good should excite us to this. Without his blessing all means are without efficacy and every effort for revival will be in vain. Constantly and earnestly, therefore, let us approach his throne. Take all occasions especially for closet prayer; here, if anywhere, we shall get fresh strength and maintain a life of communion with God. Our Lord Jesus used frequently to retire into a mountain alone for prayer, he, therefore, that is a follower of Christ, must follow him in this important duty.[47]

Now, the year before Fuller wrote these words, regular meetings for prayer had begun, which met for one specific object: to pray for biblical revival. The impact of this prayer will be explored in our next chapter.

---

46. Fuller, *Causes of Declension* (*Works*, 3:320).
47. Fuller, *Causes of Declension* (*Works*, 3:324).

CHAPTER 9

"The Lord Is Doing Great Things, and Answering Prayer Every Where"
John Sutcliff and the Concert of Prayer for Revival

How does renewal or revival come to a Christian community or congregation? A variety of answers can be given to this important question, but, from the vantage point of church history, prayer will head the list. When God's people are driven to realize their desperate need for spiritual advance and revival, they also realize they must pray for this to happen. Only God can do the work of God, and true revival is His work. As such, they cry out to God, both corporately and singly, for God to stretch forth His arm and revive His people. A great example of this important truth can be found in the English Particular Baptist community of the eighteenth century.

Now, among the Baptist figures of this period one of the most important is also one of the least known—John Sutcliff (1752–1814), the pastor of the Baptist church in Olney, Buckinghamshire, for thirty-nine years. An extremely close friend of both Andrew Fuller and William Carey and one of the founders of the Baptist Missionary Society, Sutcliff played a central part in bringing revival to the English Particular Baptists through the medium of prayer.

Early Years in West Yorkshire
Sutcliff's early nurture in the Christian faith came through his parents, Daniel and Hannah Sutcliff, both of whom attended Rodhill End Baptist Church, not far from Hebden Bridge, Yorkshire.[1] But it was

---

1. Comparatively little research has been done on the life or theology of John Sutcliff. There is a biographical sketch by Andrew Fuller attached to his funeral sermon for Sutcliff: *The Principles and Prospects of a Servant of Christ* in *Complete Works of the Rev. Andrew Fuller*, 1:342–56. Kenneth W. H. Howard, who was pastor of Sutcliff Baptist Church in

not until 1767 or 1768, when Sutcliff was either sixteen or seventeen, that he was converted during a local revival in Wainsgate Baptist Church, where his parents worshiped on alternate weeks since there was a service at Rodhill End only every other week. The pastor of the church was John Fawcett. As we saw in an earlier chapter, Fawcett was converted through the preaching of George Whitefield and was shaped as a young Christian by the eccentric Anglican evangelical William Grimshaw.

After a couple of years under Fawcett's watchful care, Sutcliff devoted two and half years, from 1772 to May of 1774, to theological study at Bristol Baptist College. He then briefly served in two Baptist churches, one in Shrewsbury and one in Birmingham, before he entered upon what would be his life's ministry at Olney, Buckinghamshire in July 1775.

Reading Jonathan Edwards

Not long after he came to Olney, John Sutcliff began to study in earnest the writings of Jonathan Edwards (1703–1758), rightly known as the theologian of revival and described by Miklós Vetö as "the greatest Christian theologian of the eighteenth century."[2] First introduced to the writings of Edwards by John Fawcett, the works of this New England divine exercised a great influence in shaping Sutcliff's theology. Edwards's writings first gave Calvinists like Sutcliff an answer to the Enlightenment critique that divine sovereignty and human freedom are incompatible. Human beings, Edwards argued, refused to obey God not because of any natural inability. Rather, it was their affections that were enslaved and needed to be reoriented in godly directions. Then, Edwards also maintained that the duty incumbent upon all who heard the gospel was immediate repentance. As a Calvinist, Edwards upheld the utter necessity of grace in conversion. But he moved away

---

Olney from 1949–1954, wrote a fine biographical piece: "John Sutcliff of Olney," *The Baptist Quarterly* 14 (1951–1952): 304–9. See also Michael A. G. Haykin, *One Heart and One Soul: John Sutcliff of Olney, His Friends, and His Times* (Darlington, Co. Durham: Evangelical Press, 1994).

2. Miklós Vetö, "Book Reviews: *America's Theologian: A Recommendation of Jonathan Edwards*, by Robert W. Jenson," *Church History* 58 (1989): 522.

from the passive understanding of conversion that had prevailed in some seventeenth-century Calvinist quarters, and that was still very much a part of High Calvinism in the eighteenth century, and argued sinners must respond to the gospel summons without delay. The upshot of Edwardsean Calvinism was a dual commitment to revival at home and strenuous missionary endeavors abroad.[3]

It was this evangelical Calvinism of Jonathan Edwards that led Sutcliff to the conviction that certain aspects of the High Calvinism that was then regnant in many Calvinistic Baptist churches were unscriptural. For instance, similar to the situation in which Andrew Fuller found himself (as noted in the previous chapter), a number of Sutcliff's fellow pastors denied that it was the *duty* of sinners to believe in the Lord Jesus. They reasoned that since the Scriptures ascribe repentance and faith to the working of the Holy Spirit, neither of these can be regarded as duties required of sinners. In practical terms, this meant that the preaching of these pastors omitted "the free invitations of the gospel" and thus "chilled many churches to their very soul."[4] Edwards's writings particularly helped Sutcliff to be convinced of "the harmony…between the duty of ministers to call on sinners to repent and believe in Christ for salvation, and the necessity of omnipotent grace to render the call effectual."[5]

Sutcliff soon began to incorporate into his preaching these fresh insights regarding the relationship between human responsibility and divine grace. Some of his congregation, however, were deeply disturbed by what they considered to be a departure from the canons of "orthodoxy" and they began to absent themselves from the church's celebration of the Lord's Supper. But Sutcliff was not to be deterred from preaching biblical truth, and "by patience, calmness, and prudent perseverance," he eventually won over all those in this congregation who stood opposed to his theological position.

---

3. Extremely helpful in summarizing Edwards's thought in this paragraph has been David W. Kling, "The New Divinity and the Origins of the American Board of Commissioners for Foreign Missions," *Church History* 72 (2003): 799–807.

4. Susannah Spurgeon and J. W. Harrald, *C. H. Spurgeon's Autobiography* (London: Passmore and Alabaster, 1899), 1:310.

5. Fuller, *Principles and Prospects* (*Works*, 1:350).

Sutcliff's commitment to Edwardsean Calvinism was shared by a number of other pastors in the geographical vicinity of Olney. In particular this included John Ryland, Jr., at College Street Baptist Church in Northampton, whom Sutcliff had met in the early 1770s, and Andrew Fuller, whom Sutcliff first met in 1776 at the annual meeting of the Northamptonshire Association, to which the churches of all three pastors belonged. In the spring of 1784, Ryland shared with Sutcliff and Fuller a treatise of Edwards which had been sent to him by the Scottish Presbyterian minister John Erskine (1721–1803). When Erskine was in his mid-twenties he had entered into correspondence with Edwards and long after Edwards's death in 1758 he had continued to uphold Edwards's theological perspectives and heartily recommend his books. Well described as "the paradigm of Scottish evangelical missionary interest through the last half of the eighteenth century,"[6] Erskine regularly corresponded with Ryland from 1780 until his death in 1803, sending him not only letters, but also, on occasion, bundles of interesting books and tracts which he sought to promote. Thus it was in April 1784 that Erskine mailed to Ryland a copy of Edwards's *Humble Attempt*. The *Humble Attempt* had not been widely heeded during the lifetime of its author. Its greatest impact came after Edwards's death. As Iain H. Murray has noted, it is arguable that no such tract on the hidden source of all true evangelistic success, namely, prayer for the Spirit of God, has ever been so widely used as this one.[7]

The Prayer Call of 1784

Reading Edwards's *Humble Attempt* in the spring of 1784 had a profound impact on Ryland, Fuller, and Sutcliff. Fuller was to preach that June at the annual meeting of the Northamptonshire Association. On his way to the meeting at Nottingham, Fuller found that heavy rains had flooded several spots of the roads over which he had to travel.

---

6. J. A. De Jong, *As the Waters Cover the Sea: Millennial Expectations in the Reformation Today Rise of Anglo-America Missions, 1640–1810* (Kampen, The Netherlands: J. H. Kok N.V., 1970), 166. On Erskine, see Jonathan M. Yeager, *Enlightened Evangelicalism: The Life and Thought of John Erskine* (Oxford: Oxford University Press, 2011).

7. Murray, *Jonathan Edwards*, 299.

At one particular point the flooded area appeared so deep that Fuller was reluctant to continue. A resident of the area who knew how deep the water actually was encouraged him to urge his horse through the water. "Go on sir," he said, "you are quite safe." As the water came up to Fuller's saddle, Fuller began to have second thoughts about continuing. "Go on, sir," the man said again, "all is right." Taking the man at his word, Fuller continued and safely traversed the flooded area of the road. This experience prompted Fuller not to preach the sermon he had planned to preach. Instead, he spoke on 2 Corinthians 5:7 at the Association meeting: "We walk by faith, not by sight."[8]

During the course of this sermon, Fuller clearly revealed the impression that Edwards's *Humble Attempt* had made upon his thinking when he appealed thus to his hearers:

> Let us take encouragement, in the present day of small things, by looking forward, and hoping for better days. Let this be attended with earnest and united prayer to Him by whom Jacob must arise. A life of faith will ever be a life of prayer. O brethren, let us pray much for an outpouring of God's spirit upon our ministers and churches, and not upon those only of our own connection and denomination, but upon "all that in every place call upon the name of Jesus Christ our Lord, both theirs and ours" (1 Cor. 1:2).[9]

At the same meeting, Sutcliff proposed that the churches of the association establish monthly prayer meetings for the outpouring of God's Holy Spirit and the consequent revival of the churches of Great Britain. This proposal was adopted by the representatives of the sixteen churches at the meeting, and on the last page of the circular letter sent out that year to the churches of the Association there was what has come to be known as "The Prayer Call of 1784," which was most likely drawn up by Sutcliff.[10] The entire document runs as follows:

---

8. Andrew Fuller, *The Nature and Importance of Walking by Faith* (*Works*, 1:117, note *).
9. Fuller, *Walking by Faith* (*Works*, 1:131).
10. [John Sutcliff], "The Prayer Call of 1784," attached to John Ryland, Jr., *The Nature, Evidences, and Advantages, of Humility* (Circular Letter of the Northamptonshire Association, 1784), 12. For a detailed study of this influential call to prayer, see especially Ernest A. Payne, *The Prayer Call of 1784* (London: Baptist Laymen's Missionary Movement, 1941); Haykin, *One Heart and One Soul*, 153–71.

Upon a motion being made to the ministers and messengers of the associate Baptist churches assembled at Nottingham, respecting meetings for prayer, to bewail the low estate of religion, and earnestly implore a revival of our churches, and of the general cause of our Redeemer, and for that end to wrestle with God for the effusion of his Holy Spirit, which alone can produce the blessed effect, it was unanimously *Resolved*, to recommend to all our churches and congregations, the spending of one hour in this important exercise, on the first Monday in every calendar month.

We hereby solemnly exhort all the churches in our connection, to engage heartily and perseveringly in the prosecution of this plan. And as it may be well to endeavour to keep the same hour, as a token of our unity herein, it is supposed the following scheme may suit many congregations, viz. to meet on the first Monday evening in May, June, and July, from 8 to 9. In Aug. from 7 to 8. Sept. and Oct. from 6 to 7. Nov. Dec. Jan. and Feb. from 5 to 6. March, from 6 to 7; and April, from 7 to 8. Nevertheless if this hour, or even the particular evening, should not suit in particular places, we wish our brethren to fix on one more convenient to themselves.

We hope also, that as many of our brethren who live at a distance from our places of worship may not be able to attend there, that as many as are conveniently situated in a village or neighbourhood, will unite in small societies at the same time. And if any single individual should be so situated as not to be able to attend to this duty in society with others, let him retire at the appointed hour, to unite the breath of prayer in private with those who are thus engaged in a more public manner.

The grand object of prayer is to be that the Holy Spirit may be poured down on our ministers and churches, that sinners may be converted, the saints edified, the interest of religion revived, and the name of God glorified. At the same time, remember, we trust you will not confine your requests to your own societies [that is, churches]; or to your own immediate connection [that is, denomination]; let the whole interest of the Redeemer be affectionately remembered, and the spread of the gospel to the most distant parts of the habitable globe be the object of your most fervent requests. We shall rejoice if *any other Christian societies* of our own or other denominations will unite with us, and do now *invite them* most cordially to join heart and hand in the attempt.

Who can tell what the consequences of such an united effort in prayer may be! Let us plead with God the many gracious promises of His Word, which relate to the future success of His gospel. He has said, "I will yet for this be enquired of by the House of Israel to do it for them, I will increase them with men like a flock." Ezek. xxxvi.37. Surely we have love enough for Zion to set apart *one hour* at a time, twelve times in a year, to seek her welfare.[11]

There are at least four noteworthy points about this Prayer Call. First, very much in evidence in this statement, as well as in the extract from Fuller's sermon, is the conviction that any reversal of the decline of the Calvinistic Baptists could not be accomplished by mere human zeal but must be effected by the Spirit of God. As Sutcliff noted in another context in strongly Edwardsean language:

> The outpouring of the divine Spirit…is the grand promise of the New Testament.… His influences are the soul, the great animating soul of all religion. These withheld, divine ordinances are empty cisterns, and spiritual graces are withering flowers. These suspended, the greatest human abilities labour in vain, and noblest efforts fall success.[12]

Then there is the catholicity that is recommended with regard to the subjects of prayer. As the Particular Baptists of the Northamptonshire Association gathered together to pray, they were encouraged not to think simply of their own churches and their own denomination, but they were to embrace in prayer believers of other denominational bodies. The kingdom of God consists of more than Particular Baptists! In fact, churches of other associations were encouraged to join with them in praying for revival. This was quite a break from earlier Baptist attitudes toward those of the established church, for example. Only thirty-five years earlier, as we noted earlier, John Gill had argued for a position that refused to countenance open Communion with Anglicans. And here this prayer call is urging prayer with them for revival. If, as is likely, Sutcliff wrote this document, the catholicity recommended is understandable from his own context in Olney, where he and the Anglican minister, who was none other than John Newton of later fame, were often in each other's company and even traded pulpits at the new year.

---

11. Ryland, Jr., *Nature, Evidences, and Advantages of Humility*, 12. Emphasis original.
12. John Sutcliff, *Jealousy for the Lord of Hosts Illustrated* (London: W. Button, 1791), 12.

Third, there is the distinct missionary emphasis of the Prayer Call. The members of the Association churches were urged to pray that the gospel be spread "to the most distant parts of the habitable globe." Little did these Baptists realize how God would begin to fulfill these very prayers within the space of less than a decade.

Finally, the sole foundation for praying for revival is located in the Scriptures. Only one text, Ezekiel 36:37, is actually cited, but those issuing this call to prayer are aware of "many gracious promises" in God's Word which speak of the successful advance of His kingdom. At first glance this passage from Ezekiel hardly seems the best text to support the Prayer Call. But the overall context of this verse needs to be considered. It is one in which God is telling Israel that He will bring them back from exile in Babylon to the promised land. Before He does this, however, He tells His people that He will stir them up to pray for this very return from exile. Sutcliff and his fellow Baptists have rightly discerned the principle that preceding times of revival and striking extensions of Christ's kingdom there invariably occur the concerted and constant prayers of Christians.

The Return of Prayers

The Association meetings at which this Prayer Call was issued were held on June 2 and 3, 1784. At the end of that month, on June 29, the church that Sutcliff pastored in Olney resolved to establish a "monthly meeting for prayer…to seek for a revival of religion."[13] Two years later, Sutcliff gave the following progress report and exhortation regarding the prayer meetings that had been established in his own church and others in the Association.

> The monthly meetings of prayer, for the general spread of the gospel, appear to be kept up with some degree of spirit. This, we hope, will yet be the case. Brethren, be not weary in well-doing, for in due time ye shall reap, if ye faint not. We learn that many other churches, in different, and some in distant parts of the land, and some of different denominations, have voluntarily acceded to the

---

13. Olney Church Book III (Sutcliff Baptist Church, Olney, Buckinghamshire), entry for June 29, 1784.

plan. We communicate the above information for your encouragement. Once more we would invite all who love truth and holiness, into whose hands our letter may fall, to unite their help. Let societies, let families, let individuals, who are friends to the cause of Christ unite with us, not only daily, but in a particular manner, at the appointed season. With pleasure we were informed of an open door in many places, for the preaching of the gospel. We request it of our friends that they would encourage the occasional ministry of the word in their respective villages and neighbourhoods, where they may be situated, to the utmost of their power. Be not backward to appear on God's side.[14]

As this text shows, Sutcliff, like his mentor Edwards, was convinced that not simply the individual prayers of God's people presaged revival, but the prayers of God's people when they gathered together to pray in unison. And, as Sutcliff went on to indicate, God was already answering their prayers by providing "an open door in many places, for the preaching of the gospel."[15]

The passing years did not diminish Sutcliff's zeal in praying for revival and stirring up such prayer. For instance, Ryland wrote in his diary for January 21, 1788:

> Brethren Fuller, Sutcliff, Carey, and I kept this day as a private fast, in my study: read the Epistles to Timothy and Titus; [Abraham] Booth's charge to [Thomas] Hopkins; [Richard] Blackerby's Life, in [John] Gillies; and [John] Rogers of Dedham's sixty Memorials for a Godly Life: and each prayed twice[16]—Carey with singular enlargement and pungency. Our chief design was to implore a revival of godliness in our own souls, in our churches, and in the church at large.[17]

---

14. John Sutcliff, *Authority and Sanctification of the Lord's Day, Explained and Enforced* (Circular Letter of the Northamptonshire Association, 1786), 1–2.

15. Sutcliff, *Authority and Sanctification of the Lord's Day*, 2.

16. These would probably have been lengthy prayers.

17. Cited in Jonathan Edwards Ryland, "Memoir of Dr. Ryland" in *Pastoral Memorials: Selected from the Manuscripts of the Late Revd. John Ryland, D. D. of Bristol* (London: B. J. Holdsworth, 1826), 1:17. Abraham Booth (1734–1806) was a well-known Baptist minister in London. His charge to Thomas Hopkins, when the latter was ordained pastor of Eagle Street Baptist Church, London, in 1785, contains the following admonition, which would not have been lost to Sutcliff and his friends: "With humility, with prayer, and with expectation, the assistance of the holy Spirit should be daily regarded," *Pastoral Cautions: An Address to the Late Mr. Thomas Hopkins* in *The Works of Abraham Booth*, ed. Michael

And in 1789, the number of prayer meetings for revival having grown considerably, Sutcliff decided to bring out an edition of Edwards's *Humble Attempt* to further encourage those meeting for prayer. Measuring only six and one quarter inches long, and three and three-quarter inches wide, and containing 168 pages, this edition was clearly designed to be a handy pocket-size edition. In his preface to this edition, Sutcliff reemphasized that the Prayer Call issued by the Northamptonshire Association five years earlier was not intended for simply Particular Baptists. Rather, they ardently wished it might become general among the real friends of truth and holiness.

> The advocates of error are indefatigable in their endeavours to overthrow the distinguishing and interesting doctrines of Christianity; those doctrines which are the grounds of our hope, and sources of our joy. Surely it becomes the followers of Christ, to use every effort, in order to strengthen the things, which remain.... In the present imperfect state, we may reasonably expect a diversity of sentiments upon religious matters. Each ought to think for himself; and every one has a right, on proper occasions, to shew [sic] his opinion. Yet all should remember, that there are but two parties in the world, each engaged in opposite causes; the cause of God and Satan; of holiness and sin; of heaven and hell. The advancement of the one, and the downfall of the other, must appear exceedingly desirable to every real friend of God and man. If such in some respects entertain different sentiments, and practice distinguishing modes of worship, surely they may unite in the above business. O for thousands upon thousands, divided into small bands in their respective cities, towns, villages, and neighbourhood, all met at the same time, and in pursuit of one end, offering up their united prayers, like so many ascending clouds of incense before the Most High!—May he shower down blessings on all the scattered tribes of Zion! Grace, great grace be with all them that love the Lord Jesus Christ in sincerity![18]

A. G. Haykin and Alison E. Haykin, (Springfield, MO: Particular Baptist Press, 2006), 1:81. Richard Blackerby (1574–1648) and John Rogers (d. 1636) were both Puritan authors. The book of John Gillies (1712–1796), the son-in-law of John McLaurin, one of the initiators of the concert of prayer in Scotland, is his *Historical Collections Relating to Remarkable Periods of the Success of the Gospel, and Eminent Instruments Employed in Promoting It*. This book is reputedly the earliest history of revivals.

18. Jonathan Edwards, preface to *An Humble Attempt to Promote Explicit Agreement and Visible Union of God's People in Extraordinary Prayer, For the Revival of Religion and the*

In this text Sutcliff positioned the Prayer Call of 1784 on the broad canvas of history, in which God and Satan are waging war for the souls of men and women. Prayer, because it is a weapon common to all who are "friends of truth and holiness," is one sphere in which Christians can present a fully united front against Satan. Sutcliff was well aware that evangelicals in his day held differing theological positions and worshiped in different ways. He himself was a convinced Baptist—convinced, for instance, that the Scriptures fully supported congregational polity and believer's baptism—yet, as he rightly emphasized in the above preface, such convictions should not prevent believers, committed to the foundational truths of Christianity, uniting together to pray for revival.

Hard on the heels of the republication of Edwards's treatise came the events leading to the formation of the Particular Baptist Society for the Propagation of the Gospel among the Heathen in 1792, later known as the Baptist Missionary Society. Included among the items recommended for prayer in the Prayer Call of 1784 had been "the spread of the gospel to the most distant parts of the habitable globe." God began to answer that specific prayer in the early 1790s. First, God provided a man with the desire to go and evangelize peoples to whom the name of Christ was completely unknown, namely, William Carey. And then the Lord gave other believers the strength and courage to support him as he went and labored. Over the next four decades Carey's example would spur numerous others to offer themselves for missionary service. Of these missionary candidates, a good number would be sent to Sutcliff to be tutored by him in a parsonage seminary that he opened at the close of the 1790s. The impact of Carey's missionary labors can be well seen in the following extract from a letter by the Anglican evangelical Thomas Scott (1747–1821), who had known Carey in his early years. Writing on December 3, 1814, to John Ryland, Scott stated:

Advancement of Christ's Kingdom on Earth, pursuant to Scripture-Promises and Prophecies concerning the Last Time (1748, Northampton: T. Dicey and Co., 1789), iv–vi.

I do most heartily rejoice in what your missionaries are doing in India. Theirs is the most regular and best conducted plan against the kingdom of darkness that modern times have shown; and I augur the most extensive success. More genuine Christian wisdom, fortitude, and disinterested assiduity, perseverance, and patience appear, than I elsewhere read of. May God protect and prosper! May all India be peopled with true Christians!—even though they be all Baptists…. The Lord is doing great things, and answering prayer every where.[19]

In 1794, two years after the formation of the Baptist Missionary Society, John Rippon (1750–1836), pastor of Carter Lane Baptist Church in Southwark, London, published a list of Particular Baptist congregations and ministers in his *Baptist Annual Register*. Rippon estimated that there were at that time 326 churches in England and fifty-six in Wales, more than double the number which had existed in 1750.[20] He printed another list of churches four years later, according to which the numbers had grown to 361 churches in England and eighty-four in Wales.[21] Reflecting on these numbers, Rippon wrote, "It is said, that more of our meeting houses have been enlarged, within the last five years, and built within the last fifteen, than had been built and enlarged for thirty years before."[22] Rippon was not exaggerating. There was indeed steady growth among the Particular Baptists during the last four decades of the eighteenth century, but it was not until the final decade of the century that there was a truly rapid influx of converts. By 1812, the number of Particular Baptist churches had risen to 532. And by 1851 it stood at over 1,370. In the words of a later writer, the Congregationalist Robert William Dale (1829–1895)—this revival had impacted his denomination as well as that of the Baptists—the effect of the revival was such that

---

19. John Scott, *Letters and Papers of the Rev. Thomas Scott* (London: L. B. Seeley and Son, 1824), 254.

20. John Rippon, "A List of the Particular Baptist Churches in England," *The Baptist Annual Register, For 1794, 1795, 1796–1797* (London, 1797), 16, 23.

21. Rippon, "List of the Particular Baptist Churches in England," *Baptist Annual Register*, 40, 42.

22. Rippon, "List of the Particular Baptist Churches in England," *Baptist Annual Register* (1801), 40.

meeting-houses which had been deserted were crowded. Meeting-houses which had been more than large enough for their congregations for two or three generations had to be made larger. New meeting-houses in great numbers were erected. Cottages were rented in villages; farm-house kitchens were lent; old barns were turned into chapels; and young men who had been hard at work all through the week at the smithy, at the carpenter's bench, or behind the counter in drapers' shops, went out in companies from the towns on Sunday mornings to conduct the services.[23]

It is surely no coincidence that preceding and accompanying this growth were the concerts of prayer that many churches had established in response to the Prayer Call of 1784.

Details of the Revival

From a more personal angle, one can observe the revival that was taking place in the following extracts from the letters of Andrew Fuller.[24] In the year 1810 Fuller noted in a letter to William Carey:

> I preached a sermon to the youth last Lord's Day from 1 Thess 2:19. I think we must have had nearly one thousand. They came from all quarters. My heart's desire and prayer for them is that they may be saved.

Fuller was still rejoicing that year when he wrote on December 28 to his close friend and fellow pastor, John Ryland, who would pen the first biography of Fuller: "I hope the Lord is at work among our young people. Our Monday and Friday night meetings are much thronged." A couple of months later he told Ryland: "The Friday evening discourses are now, and have been for nearly a year, much thronged, because they have been mostly addressed to persons under some concern about their salvation." And what was happening in Fuller's church was happening in Baptist causes throughout the length and breadth of England and Wales.

---

23. R. W. Dale, *The Old Evangelicalism and the New* (London: Hodder and Stoughton, 1889), 14.

24. The following extracts from the letters of Andrew Fuller are all cited by Doyle L. Young, "The Place of Andrew Fuller in the Developing Modern Missions Movement" (PhD thesis, Southwestern Baptist Theological Seminary, 1981), 232.

Doing Good Works

Another fruit of the revival was an emphasis on the doing of good works in contrast with the Antinomianism that had often gone hand in hand with High Calvinism. Baptists became engaged in a host of philanthropic enterprises: establishing orphanages; providing organized support for the poor and destitute, war widows, and immigrants; striving to make such barbarous sports as bearbaiting and bullbaiting illegal. Probably the best example of Baptist social action in the eighteenth century is the titanic struggle that they and other evangelicals waged first against the slave trade and then against slavery itself. It is well known that such Baptists as William Knibb (1803–1845), Thomas Burchell (1799–1846), and James Phillippo (1798–1879) were heavily involved in securing the emancipation of the slaves in the 1830s. But Particular Baptists also played a role in the earlier ending of the slave trade. In 1788, for example, at a meeting of church representatives of the Western Association, it was agreed to "express our deepest abhorrence of the Slave Trade, and to recommend it earnestly to the ministers and members of all our churches, to unite in promoting, to the utmost of our power, every scheme that is or may be proposed, to procure the abolition of a traffic so unjust, inhuman, and disgraceful."[25] Four years later, William Carey urged his fellow Baptists to give up using sugar, due to the fact that it had been produced by slave labor in the West Indies and so cleanse their "hands of blood."[26] During the entire time that Carey was in India, from 1793 till his death over forty years later, he regularly pled with God in prayer for the destruction of slavery. Apparently, no public issue exercised him more. When the emancipation of the slaves finally took place in 1833, his eyes filled with tears as he gave thanks to God and proposed that for

---

25. Cited in J. G. Fuller, *A Brief History of the Western Association* (Bristol, 1843), 55–56.

26. William Carey, *An Enquiry into the Obligations of Christians to Use Means for the Conversion of the Heathens* (1792, Didcot, Oxfordshire: The Baptist Missionary Society, 1991), 111. For a mention of this boycott of slave-grown sugar, see Charles Colson with Ellen Santilli Vaughn, *Kingdoms in Conflict* (New York, NY: William Morrow & Co., Inc.; Grand Rapids: Zondervan, 1987), 103.

an entire month the Serampore mission should give special thanksgiving to God in all of their meetings.[27]

"I Wish I Had Prayed More"

On the fiftieth anniversary of the founding of the Baptist Missionary Society, F. A. Cox, reflecting on the origins of the Society, stated that:

> The primary cause of the missionary excitement in Carey's mind, and its diffusion among the Northamptonshire ministers [was]… the meeting of the Association in 1784, at Nottingham, [when] it was resolved to set apart an hour on the first Monday evening of every month, "for extraordinary prayer for revival of religion, and for the extending of Christ's kingdom in the world." This suggestion proceeded from the venerable Sutcliff. Its simplicity and appropriateness have since recommended it to universal adoption; and copious showers of blessing from on high have been poured forth upon the churches.[28]

From the vantage point of the early 1840s, Cox saw the Prayer Call of 1784 as pivotal in that it focused the prayers of Particular Baptist churches in the Northamptonshire Association on the nations of the world, and thus prepared the way for the emergence of the Baptist Missionary Society and the sending of Carey to India. Yet he also noted that the "universal adoption" of the concert of prayer by churches beyond the ranks of the Particular Baptist denomination had led to rich times of revival, when God poured forth upon these churches "copious showers of blessing." Later historians would describe this period of blessing as the Second Evangelical Awakening (1790s–1830s). Some of them, like J. Edwin Orr and Paul E. G. Cook, would concur with Cox and rightly trace the human origins of this time of revival and spiritual awakening to the adoption of the concert of prayer by the Particular Baptists in 1784.[29]

---

27. See Ernest A. Payne, *Freedom in Jamaica: Some Chapters in the Story of the Baptist Missionary Society*, rev. ed. (London: The Carey Press, 1946), 43.

28. F. A. Cox, *History of the Baptist Missionary Society, From 1792 to 1842* (London: T. Ward & Co.; G. & J. Dyer, 1842), 1:10–11.

29. J. Edwin Orr, *The Eager Feet: Evangelical Awakenings 1790–1830* (Chicago: Moody Press, 1975), 95, 191–92, 199; Paul E. G. Cook, "The Forgotten Revival" in *Preaching and Revival* (London: The Westminster Conference, 1984), 92.

However, in one area Cox's statement is somewhat misleading. In describing Sutcliff as "the venerable Sutcliff" he leaves the reader with an idyllic impression of the Baptist pastor. How sobering to find that this man, who was at the heart of a prayer movement that God used to bring so much spiritual blessing to his church, also struggled when it came to prayer. When Sutcliff lay dying in 1814, he said to Fuller: "I wish I had prayed more."[30] For some time Fuller ruminated on this statement by his dying friend. Eventually he came to the conviction that Sutcliff did not mean that he "wished he had prayed more frequently, more *spiritually*." Then Fuller elaborated on this interpretation by applying Sutcliff's statement to his own life:

> I wish I had prayed more for the influence of the Holy Spirit; I might have enjoyed more of the power of vital godliness. I wish I had prayed more for the assistance of the Holy Spirit, in studying and preaching my sermons; I might have seen more of the blessing of God attending my ministry. I wish I had prayed more for the outpouring of the Holy Spirit to attend the labours of our friends in India; I might have witnessed more of the effects of their efforts in the conversion of the heathen.[31]

Whether or not Fuller correctly interpreted Sutcliff's statement, his application certainly resonates with themes dear to Sutcliff's heart: personal renewal, the revival of the church, and Spirit-empowered prayer and witness.

---

30. Fuller, *Principles and Prospects* (*Works*, 1:344).

31. Cited in J. W. Morris, *Memoirs of the Life and Writings of the Rev. Andrew Fuller* (London, 1816), 443.

CONCLUSION

Eight Theses on Revival

*1. The History of the Church is a History
of Revival and Times of Declension.*
In this respect, the book of Judges seems to be emblematic of the history of the church. There are times of declension when God's people trust in anything but the Spirit of the Lord to do the work of God. The church in such times languishes in weakness until she cries out to God, "Will You not revive us again?" There follow times of flourishing, when the church is teeming with vigor and power, and there is a conscious dependence upon the might of the Spirit of God.

2. Revival Is a Work Grounded in the Sovereignty of the Holy Spirit.
Revival—the breathing of new life into the church—is a divine work of grace. It cannot be accomplished by mere human zeal and ingenuity. If it were possible for men and women to revive the church by their own innate energy and will power, what need would there be of the Spirit of God in our midst? The outpouring of the Holy Spirit upon the disciples at Pentecost is our model here: wait in Jerusalem, their Lord told them, "until ye be endued with power from on high" (Luke 24:49).

*3. When God Determines to Revive His Church, He Begins
by Stirring up His People to Pray for What He Will Do.*
The fact that revival is a work of the Holy Spirit does not mean that in times of declension, God's people can sit back, do nothing, and wait

for the Spirit to act. No, they are called and indeed energized to pray for revival and to repent of their sins and spiritual lethargy.[1]

4. Times of Revival Are Attended by a Solid Commitment to the Bible as the Word of the Living God, Infallible and Unerring.
The Scriptures have been created by the Holy Spirit, who has breathed them into existence (2 Tim. 3:16). During those times when His work of regeneration and sanctification is so remarkable, it is unthinkable that the Bible, by which He saves sinners and sanctifies them (James 1:18; John 17:17) should be held as anything but what it is: the Holy Word of God.

5. Genuine Revival Is Always Attended with Faithful Preaching of the Scriptures.
The Word of God is the great instrument of conversion and sanctification (see Heb. 4:12–13), not human oratory and eloquence, nor the sacraments (important as these are in the life of the church), nor the pattern of worship. It is the Word of God in the hand of its author, the Holy Spirit, that convicts, illumines, liberates, regenerates, and rejoices the heart.

6. Revival Is Accompanied by Theological Renewal, for the Holy Spirit Is Ever the Spirit of Truth.
The Holy Spirit, who is the leading agent of revival, is ever the Spirit of truth (John 14:17; 16:13). When He comes in power to revive His people, He takes them back to the truth of His Word and there is theological renewal and even degrees of reformation.

7. Spirit-Wrought Revival Always Impacts the Societal Context of the Churches That Are Being Renewed and Revitalized.
Revival cannot be contained within the four walls of Christian congregations. As the hearts of God's people are revived and stirred

---

1. See Brian H. Edwards, *Praying for Revival* (Leominster, UK: Day One Publications, 2019).

afresh, they engage in evangelism and mission to those outside of their communities. They engage in good works, which leads to significant streams of blessing.

8. Revival Is a Christ-Centered Experience.
The central feature of the new-covenant ministry of the Holy Spirit is the glorification of Jesus Christ (John 16:14). As a work of the Holy Spirit, revival then is first and foremost a time when Jesus Christ is set forth in all of His glory as Savior and Lord.

APPENDIX 1

William Grimshaw's Letter on the Haworth Revival

William Grimshaw left very little by way of written material, which makes the following letter that he wrote to John Gillies, the Scottish chronicler of revival, quite significant. It is dated July 19, 1754, and was written to Gillies by Grimshaw from Haworth.

In the year 1738, our gracious Redeemer was pleased to revive his work in the West Riding, as we call it, of this county of York. Now were poor souls amongst us brought to know Jesus alone, for their wisdom, righteousness, sanctification, and redemption. The first instrument sent hither by our dear Immanuel, was one Mr. Benjamin Ingham, a clergyman, and one of the Oxford Methodists. He was born at Osset,[1] in this Riding. The clergy at first received him into their pulpits, the churches were soon crowded, and a great stirring up of the people to seek salvation by faith alone, in the merits of a crucified Saviour, quickly appeared. But Satan, perceiving his kingdom to be in danger, began to roar, and the clergy (as I have been informed) were forbid to receive Mr. Ingham any more. Wakefield, Osset, Leeds, Halifax, and many other churches and chapels he preached in, until he was prohibited. And greatly were the people blessed. He then betook himself (as did Messrs Wesleys, Whitefield, and others at the same time) to our Saviour's manner, field preaching. As eminently did our Lord soon testify that this was his good pleasure. Multitudes assembled everywhere, and it soon appeared that conscience rather than curiosity was the main motive thereto. Man's fall and degeneracy, his redemption

---

1. The contemporary spelling is Ossett.

through Christ Jesus alone, the nature and necessity of the new birth, justification by faith only, sanctification by the indwelling Spirit of our redeemer, etc., these were (and still are) the main doctrines and subjects of all discourse. Many people not only heard, but were convinced, converted, and brought to a saving, experimental knowledge of these truths. The kingdom of God soon appeared to be a kingdom within by righteousness, and peace, and joy in the Holy Ghost.... In 1742...our dear Lord was pleased to visit my parish (Haworth). A few souls were affected under the Word, brought to see their lost estate by nature and to experience peace through faith in the blood of Jesus. My church began to be crowded, insomuch that many were obliged to stand out of doors. Here, as in other places, it was amazing to hear and see what weeping, roaring, and agonies many people were seized with at the apprehension of their sinful state and the wrath of God. After a season, I joined people (such as were truly seeking, or had found the Lord) in society for the exercises [of praying, singing, reading, conferring together about the work of God in their souls].... These meetings here, as it is all over the kingdom, it may be your desire to understand, are held once a week, about two hours, and are called classes consisting of about ten or twelve members each. We have much of the Lord's presence among them; and greatly, in consequence, must such meetings conduce to Christian edification. Not unto me, not unto me, but to the Lord Jesus's name solely be the praise....

What you here receive is a brief relation of the work of God in these parts of this kingdom. I suppose our brethren, particularly Mr. [John] Wesley and Mr. Whitefield, have furnished you with accounts from every other part where it hath appeared. I have only the following observations to make to you:

1. That, soon after the devil observed such crying and distress of soul and agitation of body to affect people under the Word, he also began to seize people under the Word with strange unnatural distortions, convulsions, hideous roarings, to bring, as we plainly saw, contempt and disgrace upon the true work of God. For it is remarkable that the

generality of such persons, whatsoever pretence of repentance they might then make, dwindled away to nothing.

2. That, for seven years past, the cryings and agitations in sincere penitents are in a manner ceased and are rarely seen *or* heard of. The Lord Jesus now carries on his work in the heart in a still serious affecting way, and I trust with as great success as ever since it began.

3. That in most places where the Gospel has been purely preached, it still flourishes, congregations increase, and doors are continually opening. Come and help us is the common cry.

4. That out of our Societies the Lord hath raised up many to preach the Gospel. None of them *called thereto*, but such only as are experimentally born again, and pardoned, and know the Lord Jesus Christ to be in them the hope of glory. Those speak, as our Lord says, *that* they do know. They speak from the heart to the heart. Their labours are wonderfully blessed. And such are God's chief instruments employed in carrying on the present wonderful work.

5. That, whereas this work took place at first mainly among the illiterate, poor, and vulgar, it, of late, has gained the credit and esteem of the more wealthy, wise, and learned sort of people. Many such, in most places, are come to experience the life, peace, and power of Christ Jesus in their souls. That so it is, is well for them indeed; but whether it presage well to the future prosperity of this work I will not say.

6. That at the first coming of the Gospel to any place, it generally happens that Satan roars, and mobs and riots are stirred up; but however violent, the Lord seldom suffers much harm to be done to his people; quietness is soon procured, and his Word *takes place*....

Thus, you have the substance of what I can inform you of. May our very dear Saviour be with you and yours forever. Pray for me and I'll pray for you. W. G.[2]

---

2. This letter can be found in John Gillies, *Historical Collections of Accounts of Revival* (1845, Edinburgh: Banner of Truth, 1981), 506–8.

APPENDIX 2

John Stutterd, "The Means of Reviving and Promoting Religion"

John Stutterd (ca. 1750–1818) was the founding pastor of the Baptist Church in the market town of Colne, Lancashire, from its formation in 1769 till his death. He was remembered as "a man of considerable biblical knowledge."[1] This circular letter on the revitalization of local churches was published by the Yorkshire and Lancashire Association of Particular Baptist churches in 1795 and appears to have been his sole published work.[2] To enable the use of this text as a study guide for revival, I have appended a number of questions about the text following it.

Dear Brethren,

The religion which you profess is not a cunningly devised fable. Its truth is attested by evidences which an honest mind cannot resist. The heavens declare the being and glory of God; and the firmament sheweth his handiwork. Day unto day, and night unto night, display the knowledge of his wisdom, goodness, and power. Your own observation and experience corroborate the testimony of the Bible, concerning the fall, depravity, and guilt of mankind. And the good-tidings of redemption, by which sinners are encouraged to return to God, in hopes of pardon, acceptance, and life, are, without reasonable

---

1. "Deaths," *The Gentleman's Magazine: and Historical Chronicle* 88, part 2 (July–December 1818): 88. On Stutterd, see also Percy Stock, "John Stutterd of Colne," *The Baptist Quarterly* 6 (1931–1932): 227–31; and Dora Yates, *The Baptist In Colne* (Colne, Lancashire, 1985), 8–13.

2. John Stutterd, *The Means of Reviving and Promoting Religion* (Circular Letter of the Yorkshire and Lancashire Association, 1795), 16 pages. In the reproduction of this text, punctuation has been modernized and the text has been slightly edited.

doubt, the glorious gospel of the blessed God. Herein the ancient prophecies are evidently fulfilled. The miracles of Jesus exhibit his power as the Messiah and his kindness as the Prince of Peace. The rapid progress of the gospel in the apostolic age is a striking testimony to its truth. The primitive preachers combated the prejudices, pride, policy, and power of a self-sufficient, wicked world, and they were gloriously successful. The weapons of their warfare were not carnal. They went forth in the power of the Spirit of God. The hand of the Lord was with them, and, through him, they prospered. The doctrines of your holy religion approve themselves to every unprejudiced enquirer: being manifestly worth of its sovereign, wise, and gracious Author. They are just to God, safe for man. Its precepts are pure and good. Its threatenings righteously agitate our fears, and its promises mercifully inspire our hopes of grace, more grace, final acceptance, immortality, and eternal life.

If, as we trust, this divine religion hath come unto you not in word only, but in power, you have viewed and felt its excellent nature and vast importance. It hath, according to the degree of its influence, enlightened your understandings, pacified your consciences, and purified your hearts. The truly religious know God and love him. They fear him and think upon his name. Sin is their sorrow and Christ is their hope. Through him, the Way, they draw near unto, serve and worship the Father, by the gracious assistance of the Holy Spirit. Governed by religion, you have a regard to God in all you do. His Word is your rule; his glory is your end. Thereby, you are taught submission to his ordinances; to do to others, as ye would they should do to you; and, as you have opportunity, to do good unto all men, especially to them who are of the household of faith. "Pure religion and undefiled before God and the Father is this, to visit the fatherless and widows in their affliction, and to keep himself unspotted from the world."[3]

Real religion is the one thing needful. Many things are valuable; but this is the principal. Destitute of this, whatever we possess, we are wretched and miserable, and poor, and blind, and naked; having no

---

3. James 1:27.

well-grounded hope; and being without Christ, and without God in the world. Our privileges are perverted; we are hurtful to our connections. Sin and Satan are our masters; and dreadful is the end which awaits us. On the contrary, the people are blessed who know the joyful sound, whose God is the Lord, who fear him, and walk in his ways. For Christ is their life; God is their Father; the Holy Spirit is their Guide and Comforter. Their afflictions on earth are mercies in disguise: and heaven shall be their eternal portion. "Godliness is profitable unto all things, having promise of the life that now is, and of that which is to come."[4]

With such views of religion, every benevolent mind must lament its present circumstances among men. By multitudes of every rank it is openly opposed, despised, or neglected. And there is reason to fear that many who profess to be its friends are not duly attentive to its interests. We are much affected with the low and divided state of Christianity in general; and would gladly, in our humble spheres, be instrumental of promoting the union and prosperity of all its genuine friends. But we have nearer concerns. Primitive religion is languid among ourselves. There is a declension in its energy and life. The humility, diligence, affection, and godly simplicity of the first Christians rarely appear. The Holy Spirit is grieved; and little success attends the preaching of the Word. May we lay these things closely to heart! They require the immediate attention of ministers and people. We, therefore, propose to lay before you, in this letter, a few thoughts on the most likely means for the revival and promotion of vital and practical religion in our churches and congregations. Accordingly, we desire your close, and candid attention to the following things, which we apprehend to be of that description.

1. Serious consideration on the evil nature of sin. It is hateful to God, and pernicious to man. Wherever it obtains, the progress of that which is good is impeded. There cannot be the shadow of a doubt that sin is the cause of declensions in religion. If this be indulged, spiritual health and vigour decay. For instance, do not sensual gratifications take the heart from divine things? "Fleshly lusts…war against the

---

4. 1 Tim. 4:8.

soul."[5] They are in arms against its purity and prosperity. Again, can that person thrive in the means of grace, who entertains and undue solicitude respecting earthly things? We may as reasonably expect corn to come to maturity which is overgrown with briars and thorns. "The care of this world, and the deceitfulness of riches, choke the word, and he becometh unfruitful."[6] Farther, is not unnecessary communion with carnal men detrimental to our best interests? We think lamentable experience hath often proved it. Thereby we are exposed to many temptations. And, perhaps, before we are apprized of our danger, we assimilate to their spirit, manners, and customs. "Be not conformed to this world: but be ye transformed by the renewing of your mind."[7] Brethren, mark these things as dangerous enemies to your peace, usefulness, and prosperity. And remember that every allowed sin is inconsistent therewith. Search and try your ways. Enquire into the particular causes of declension in your own souls or in your societies. And, whatever they be, lament and forsake them. If these remain, the effect will not be removed. "If I regard iniquity in my heart, the Lord will not hear me."[8] "Your iniquities have separated between you and your God."[9] "Therefore…now, saith the LORD, turn ye even to me with all your heart, and with fasting, and with weeping, and with mourning. And rend your heart, and not your garments, and turn unto the LORD your God: for he is gracious and merciful, slow to anger, and of great kindness."[10]

2. We add reflection upon the love of Christ. This appears abundantly in what he hath done for his church. He became surety for us in the everlasting covenant; and in the fullness of time, though he was rich, for our sakes he became poor, that we, through his poverty, might be rich. He loved us and gave himself on the cross an offering and a sacrifice for us; dying, the just for the unjust, that he might deliver us

---

5. Cf. 1 Peter 2:11.
6. Matt. 13:22.
7. Rom. 12:2.
8. Ps. 66:18.
9. Isa. 59:2.
10. Joel 2:12–13.

from wrath, and bring us to God. Will not attentive consideration of his death, soften our hard hearts and enkindle our repentings for sin? Let us think, how he endured the cross that in trials, for his sake, we be not weary and faint in our minds. Let us remember the expense at which he purchased his church, and, surely, it will induce us not to think any thing too much, which we can do, to promote the interests of Zion. In reflecting on his propitiatory sacrifice, with which the Father is well pleased, we are encouraged to return unto God from our declensions and are excited to a becoming walk, the love of Christ constraining us to live unto him, who died for us. Here is a fountain opened to us for sin and uncleanness. Therefore, when sin defiles our consciences, let us not wear it off by time, for this is very dangerous; but wash it away by application to this fountain. The blood of Jesus Christ, the Son of God, cleanseth us from all sin.

3. Farther, we recommend the diligent and proper use of the divine Word. Its Author hath magnified it above all his name; and, if we know its worth and importance, we shall magnify it too. The Holy Scriptures are able to make wise unto salvation, through faith in Christ. By them we are quickened, strengthened, comforted, and preserved in the path of life. The neglect or improper use of God's Word is a very probable cause of the languishing state of vital godliness, of which we complain. For thence proceed instability of mind, lukewarmness, and irregularity of conduct. Our having it in plenty, may be an occasion of it being slighted. However, let us see that this be not the case henceforth. Brethren, read the Scriptures diligently. They are a valuable mine; but it must be worked. Meditate upon what you read and pray over it. A blessing is pronounced upon the man, who delights in the law of the Lord, and meditates therein day and night. "He shall be like a tree planted by the rivers of water, that bringeth forth his fruit in his season."[11] Read the Scriptures to form your sentiments— to correct your mistakes, in faith or practice, and that you may know what is that good, and perfect, and acceptable will of God. They have been the grand means of revival in the church of God in former times.

---

11. Ps. 1:3.

Of this we have illustrious instances. Josiah, the king of Judah, was a pious reformer. He set his heart to restore the purity of religion; and this good work was greatly promoted, by the affectionate reading of the book of the law. In the days of Ezra and Nehemiah there was a pleasing revival, of which the Word of God was evidently the principal means. For we learn that Ezra, and his companions, stood upon a pulpit of wood, read the law, and gave the meaning; and the people understood the law, wept bitterly, and entered into a covenant with their God. The blessed Reformation, which took place in Europe in the sixteenth century, is another bright example. The Scriptures were translated and preached; the common people heard them, read them, and highly esteemed them. These were the principal means of effecting the glorious work. The darkness of Popery fled before the light of Scripture. The Word of the Lord was precious in those days.[12] May it be precious to us! May we, through the divine blessing, find it spirit and life to our souls!

4. Again, we mention the careful cultivation of divine religion in your families. Whatever be the relation in which you stand, punctually discharge your duties and endeavour to promote the order and piety of the household. But herein parents and masters are especially concerned. It is their bounden duty, to maintain the worship of God in their families; to instruct the rising generation in the principles of religion; to watch over their morals and to inure[13] them to constant attendance on the public service of the house of God. And this

---

12. "When Archbishop Cranmer's edition of the Bible was printed, in 1538, and fixed to a desk in all parochial churches, the ardour with which men flocked to read it, is incredible. They who could, procured it, and they who could not, crowded to read it, or to hear it read in churches; where it was common to see little assemblies of mechanics meeting together for that purpose, after the labour of the day. Many even learned to read in their old age, that they might have the pleasure of instructing themselves from the Scriptures. Mr. Fox mentions two apprentices, who joined each his little flock, and brought a Bible; which, at every interval of leisure, they read; but being afraid of their master, who was a zealous papist, they kept it under the straw of their bed. Such was the extasy of joy with which this blessing was received at that time, when it was uncommon." This is Stutterd's footnote. The precise bibliographical reference has been added: William Gilpin, *The Life of Thomas Cranmer, Archbishop of Canterbury* (London: R. Blamire, 1784), 62–63.

13. A positive use of the term "inure," which today normally has a negative connotation.

should be attended to with hearty concern, that those under their care may have the power, with the form of religion. Use your utmost endeavours, in dependence upon the blessing of God. He encourages you to hope that your labour shall not be in vain. "Train up a child in the way he should go: and when he is old, he will not depart from it."[14] We greatly fear there is a remissness among us in this important matter. And then no wonder, if our churches decline. To them our families should be as the nursery to the plantation. If children, and young persons, are suffered to herd with vain companions, and roam at large in search of their own pleasure on the sabbath-day, what can be expected? They contract evil habits; and the ways of Zion mourn, God is dishonoured; your hearts are pained; and the object of your prayers and instructions is frustrated. In some instances, we think, much injury is done to the cause, by parents indulging an idea of its being well, if their children attend public worship anywhere. For hence, they are permitted to ramble. This alienates their minds from our assemblies; and may often be a cloak for sabbath-breaking. We should make it an indispensable point, that they worship God with us; unless there appears against it, principle of conscience. "As for me and my house, we will serve the LORD."[15] "I know Abraham, that he will command his children and his household after him; and they shall keep the way of the LORD, to do justice and judgment."[16]

5. Farther, we specify the filling up your places in the church with constancy. Of your obligation to this, there can be no doubt. Your relation to the church, the divine command, and the example of the primitive saints, shew it evidently. Therefore, you should be conscientious in it as an incumbent duty. Were everyone so, the interests of Zion would wear a hopeful aspect. It is a likely mean for the revival of our own souls. "They that wait upon the LORD shall renew their strength."[17] His Word doth good to them, who walk uprightly. Steadfast in our places,

---

14. Prov. 22:6.
15. Josh. 24:15.
16. Cf. Gen. 18:19.
17. Isa. 40:31.

we strengthen and revive one another. "Iron sharpeneth iron; so a man sharpeneth the countenance of his friend."[18] Your presence in the assembly, is more cheering to your pastors, than that of strangers, as you are the objects of their more immediate care. "Now we live, if ye stand fast in the Lord."[19] We therefore entreat you, not to suffer any temporal employ or sensual gratification—any unnecessary journey, or formal visit, to take you from your duty and privilege in the church of God. These must be displeasing to him, as contrary to the law of his house; and also, as breaches of his holy sabbath. "Remember the sabbath day, to keep it holy."[20] If this is neglected, religion will droop. How is your practice in this respect? This is the duty which the Lord hath particularly appointed, for his own honour, the promotion of his kingdom, and our spiritual advantage. May we employ every part of it as sacred to these purposes! Our sanctification of the sabbath, and the revival of the church, are closely connected. "If thou turn away thy foot from the sabbath, from doing thy pleasure on my holy day; and call the sabbath a delight, the holy of the LORD, honourable; and shalt honour him, not doing thine own ways, nor finding thine own pleasure, nor speaking thine own words: Then shalt thou delight thyself in the LORD; and I will cause thee to ride upon the high places of the earth, and feed thee with the heritage of Jacob thy father: for the mouth of the LORD hath spoken it."[21]

You have places in church-meetings. How are they filled? What pity, you should be ever unnecessarily absent! For here your presence, and assistance are particularly needful, to encourage and manage discipline, order, and general concerns of the house of God. If these are neglected, the church cannot prosper. And, though your officers may be justly expected to take a leading part, you are all intimately concerned. Let the purity, peace, and honour of the church, lie near your hearts, and contribute all in your power to the promotion of them. If

---

18. Prov. 27:17.
19. 1 Thess. 3:8.
20. Ex. 20:8.
21. Isa. 58:13–14.

we connive at sin, under any consideration, how can we expect the presence of God? Holiness becometh his house for ever.

6. Again, we recommend the exercise of mutual brotherly kindness. We trust, ye have purified your souls in obeying the truth through the Spirit unto unfeigned love of the brethren; see then that ye love one another, with pure hearts, fervently. Pray for each other; and speak often one to another. Sympathize with each other in affliction; and admonish one another in times of dangers. By love serve one another in things spiritual and temporal. This will knit your hearts together in the ways of God, for charity is the bond of perfectness. Hereby you have evidence that you are born of God and will manifest that you are disciples of Christ indeed. This will render your meetings comfortable and your profession amiable. It is a very likely mean of promoting the cause of your Redeemer. Where brethren dwell together in unity, the Lord commandeth the blessing. "Be of one mind, live in peace; and the God of love and peace shall be with you."[22]

7. We add, care to encourage your ministers, in their important work. On them as instruments, in some measure depend the revival and progress of religion among you. But they are encompassed with infirmity, are men of like passions with yourselves. All their sufficiency is of God. Let them have a constant interest in your addresses to the throne of grace. Be earnestly desirous that they may have light in their studies and liberty in their pulpits—that their hearts may be in their work—that they may speak boldly as they ought to speak—and that their word may be clothed with power to the hearts of saints and sinners. Encourage them to visit you at your own houses; and to be free and open in conversation for your spiritual good. Communicate unto them the state of your minds. This will assist them in the choice of their subjects and management of their public discourses. Encourage them to converse with and catechize your children. This will assist you in forming their minds and may be productive of much good. Lectures in the neighbourhood on Lord's-day evenings and at other

---

22. 2 Cor. 13:11.

suitable seasons seem very likely to be useful: encourage your ministers in this labour, by opening your own houses, or endeavouring to find other places proper for this purpose.

8. Moreover, we particularly recommend a general conversation becoming the gospel. For if your lives are immoral, the cause will be covered with reproach—the pious will be grieved—the weak will be stumbled, and your meeting houses avoided. See then, that ye walk circumspectly. Be chaste, sober, peaceable, and honest—studious to have a good report of all men and of the truth itself. Thus, you will stop the mouths of gainsayers, and prove that salvation by sovereign grace is a doctrine according to godliness. "Let your light so shine before men, that they may see your good works, and glorify your Father which is in heaven."[23]

9. Lastly, we urge persevering, fervent prayer. Mourning our low estate, let us seek to the Lord for revival. When Jacob is small, by whom shall he arise, but by his God. It is "not by might, nor by power, but by my spirit, saith the LORD of hosts."[24] He hath promised his presence, and blessings, to his churches. Yea, glorious things are spoken of the city of God. Yet, he will be enquired of, to do these things to them. Accordingly, in declining circumstances, the friends of Zion, have given themselves in prayer. "LORD, revive thy work in the midst of the years, in the midst of the years make known; in wrath remember mercy."[25] "Wilt thou not revive us again: that thy people may rejoice in thee?"[26] Do good in thy good pleasure unto Zion: build thou the walls of Jerusalem."[27] This language is recorded, for our imitation. Let us tread in this footstep of the flock. Our encouragement is great. For "thus saith the LORD, the Holy One of Israel, and his Maker, Ask me of things to come concerning my sons, and concerning the work of my hands command ye me."[28]

---

23. Matt. 5:16.
24. Zech. 4:6.
25. Hab. 3:2.
26. Ps. 85:6.
27. Ps. 51:18.
28. Isa. 45:11.

Brethren, unite, cordially unite in earnest prayer for the revival and increase of the church. Then will Zion travail and shall bring forth children. The disciples of our Lord, after his ascension, continued with one accord in prayer and supplication. Thus, they waited for the promise of the Father. The Spirit was speedily poured out from on high; and, on one day, there were added unto them about three thousand souls. The Lord still hears and answers prayer. His hand is not shortened; nor is his ear grown heavy. Suffer not disunion to hinder your prayers. Sensible of your own unworthiness, ask in the name of Christ. Seek his kingdom and righteousness in the principal place. "Ye that make mention of the LORD, keep not silence, and give him no rest, till he establish, and till he make Jerusalem a praise in the earth."[29]

We wish you to recollect and examine these ideas. As likely means for the revival and promotion of religion among you, we have pointed out—serious considerations on the evil nature of sin—reflection upon the love of Christ—the diligent and proper use of the divine Word—the cultivation of genuine religion in your families—filling up your places in the church with constancy—the exercise of mutual brother kindness—care to encourage your ministers in their important work—a general conversation becoming the gospel—and persevering, fervent prayer.

We doubt not you will receive these lines in love; and hope you will be upright and diligent in practical attention to them as far as they are agreeable to the will of God. Indeed, this highly becomes us all. For the souls of men are of inconceivable worth. Satan is vigilant, and powerful in his opposition. The bulk of mankind are active and zealous in the pursuit of transitory things. And shall we be remiss in attempting the revival and promotion of that religion, by which Satan is conquered, souls everlastingly saved, and the blessed God abundantly glorified?

"Now the God of peace, that brought again from the dead our Lord Jesus, that great shepherd of the sheep, through the blood of the everlasting covenant, make you perfect in every good work to do his

---

29. Isa. 62:6–7.

will, working in you that which is wellpleasing in his sight, through Jesus Christ; to whom be glory for ever and ever. Amen."[30]

Questions

1. What is "the one thing needful"?

2. Why is "the revival and promotion of vital and practical religion" needed?

3. The first means of revival is "serious consideration on the evil nature of sin." Why does Stutterd deem this important? What do you make of his statement about "unnecessary communion with carnal men"?

4. How can "reflection upon the love of Christ" be an aid to revival?

5. What relationship does Stutterd see between "the divine Word" and revival? How then should we act with regard to the Scriptures?

6. What is the fourth means of revival that Stutterd notes? Were you surprised to see this mentioned? Why or why not?

7. What is a fifth critical means of revival? Do you agree when Stutterd argues that "our sanctification of the sabbath, and the revival of the church, are closely connected"? Why or why not?

8. Why does Stutterd think that "the exercise of mutual brotherly kindness" is another means of revival? What practical suggestions does Stutterd make in this regard?

9. Why does Stutterd believe it is important to "encourage… ministers"?

10. The eighth means of promoting revitalization is "a general conversation becoming the gospel," by which Stutterd has in view one's life. The final means, enumerated as number nine, is "persevering, fervent prayer." What type of prayer does Stutterd have in mind, private or corporate praying? Is this significant? Why or why not?

---

30. Heb. 13:20–21.

Acknowledgments

A big thank-you to David Woollin and Dr. Joel Beeke (to whom I have dedicated this book) for asking me to write this small work on a subject that plays a large role in my thoughts and prayers. I am also indebted to Dr. Roy Paul for transcribing Appendix 2, and a big thank-you to Brooke Bryćko for her skillful editing of this book. While much of the material in this book has appeared before, I have gone over the entirety so as to revise and amplify the text of what has been published elsewhere and to unify it. I am indebted to the following publishers for permission to reproduce material from their publications:

Joshua Press: Portions of chapters 3 and 4 are taken from my *Eighteenth-Century Evangelicals as Spiritual Mentors: "Love Is Unfurled,"* The Christian Mentor, vol. 3 (Kitchener, ON: Joshua Press, 2018).

Evangelical Press: Much of chapters 5 and 6 appeared in *Jonathan Edwards: The Holy Spirit in Revival* (Darlington, Co. Durham: Evangelical Press, 2005).

Bryntirion Press: Much of chapters 7 to 9 was published in *Ardent Love to Jesus: English Baptists and the Experience of Revival in the Long Eighteenth Century* (Bryntirion, Bridgend: Bryntirion Press, 2013).